Samhain

The Ultimate Guide to Halloween and How It's Celebrated in Wicca, Druidry, and Celtic Paganism

© Copyright 2022 — All rights reserved.

The content contained within this book may not be reproduced, duplicated, or transmitted without direct written permission from the author or the publisher.

Under no circumstances will any blame or legal responsibility be held against the publisher, or author, for any damages, reparation, or monetary loss due to the information contained within this book, either directly or indirectly.

Legal Notice:

This book is copyright protected. It is only for personal use. You cannot amend, distribute, sell, use, quote, or paraphrase any part, or the content within this book, without the consent of the author or publisher.

Disclaimer Notice:

Please note the information contained within this document is for educational and entertainment purposes only. All effort has been executed to present accurate, up-to-date, reliable, complete information. No warranties of any kind are declared or implied. Readers acknowledge that the author is not engaging in the rendering of legal, financial, medical, or professional advice. The content within this book has been derived from various sources. Please consult a licensed professional before attempting any techniques outlined in this book.

By reading this document, the reader agrees that under no circumstances is the author responsible for any losses, direct or indirect, that are incurred as a result of the use of information contained within this document, including, but not limited to, errors, omissions, or inaccuracies.

Your Free Gift (only available for a limited time)

Thanks for getting this book! If you want to learn more about various spirituality topics, then join Mari Silva's community and get a free guided meditation MP3 for awakening your third eye. This guided meditation mp3 is designed to open and strengthen ones third eye so you can experience a higher state of consciousness. Simply visit the link below the image to get started.

https://spiritualityspot.com/meditation

Table of Contents

INTRODUCTION 1
CHAPTER 1: FROM SAMHAIN TO HALLOWEEN 3
CHAPTER 2: SAMHAIN DEITIES AND LORE 14
CHAPTER 3: SAMHAIN CRAFTS AND DECORATIONS 24
CHAPTER 4: SETTING UP YOUR SAMHAIN ALTAR 35
CHAPTER 5: SACRED HERBS AND PLANTS 42
CHAPTER 6: CELEBRATING WITH FOOD 51
CHAPTER 7: FAMILY AND GROUP ACTIVITIES 63
CHAPTER 8: SAMHAIN RITUALS AND CEREMONIES 72
CHAPTER 9: SPELLS, CHARMS, AND BATHS 82
CHAPTER 10: SAMHAIN PRAYERS AND BLESSINGS 94
CONCLUSION 104
HERE'S ANOTHER BOOK BY MARI SILVA THAT YOU MIGHT LIKE 106
YOUR FREE GIFT (ONLY AVAILABLE FOR A LIMITED TIME) 107
BIBLIOGRAPHY 108

Introduction

As a modern witch or Wiccan practitioner, you are likely to have heard about Samhain, or as it is more commonly known, Halloween. However, there is a big difference between the two. What is it, you may ask? You will find out in the upcoming chapters. The gist of it is that Halloween originated from Samhain. While they are very much alike, Samhain is celebrated with much more serious intensity by members of the pagan persuasion. Considered one of the biggest celebrations in pagan and Wiccan culture, Samhain brings a lot of festivities and enthusiasm to the table. While many people consider it a dark occasion, this time is a celebration to honor those who have moved on from our world.

Ancient Celts lived in fear during this time, as they believed it to have been a dark time when the connection between the land of the dead and the land of the living was at its strongest. While many of these beliefs still exist in modern cultures, fear has been replaced by curiosity and the need to honor the dead. Many people still believe that Samhain is a dark and dangerous time, where evil spirits are out in the open, looking to attack. While a smidgen of this belief may be true, people consider Samhain a celebratory event. Because of this, numerous traditions and rituals are practiced with great passion to this day.

Samhain has a rich history and folklore, making it one of the most enjoyable holidays in Wiccan and pagan cultures. Plus, its connection with Halloween makes it even more fascinating for people. The mythology surrounding Samhain and its associated gods is captivating and discussed in later chapters. The myths and legends are each more enthralling than the next. Thus, this book is perfect for people interested in pagan folklore and mythology.

Filled with detailed instructions on various crafts and decorations you can make to celebrate the season with full enthusiasm, you will not have to look elsewhere for ideas. Plus, you'll find a detailed chapter about how you can set up the sacred altar of Samhain to follow the rituals associated with the ceremony properly. Then, you'll discover how several plants and herbs associated with Samhain are used for ritualistic purposes. These plants help with the remembrance and clairvoyance process.

A grand feast follows the rituals for Samhain, which may interest you because of the unique dishes specially prepared for these festivities. You'll have to read on to find a whole chapter dedicated to Samhain meals. It's easy to read and provides step-by-step instructions on preparing certain meals.

Finally, you'll find chapters covering various activities and rituals especially reserved for the Samhain season. These include hands-on exercises with easy-to-follow instructions and details for every ritual. There are even some child-friendly rituals and activities if you want your kids to participate in this festival. So, whether you're a practicing Wiccan or a newly converted witch learning the basics of centuries-old Celtic culture, this book is suitable for all audiences.

Chapter 1: From Samhain to Halloween

While Halloween is the most popular October celebration in modern times, we can trace its roots back to the Gaelic festival of Samhain. Today, many people treat the two as interchangeable or think Samhain was essentially the "same" as Halloween.

However, this could not be further from the truth. In this book, you will learn about celebrating Samhain in its various iterations in paganism, including Wicca, Druidry, and Celtic paganism. However, before you can start celebrating, you should first understand Samhain's history and traditions.

Understanding Samhain

Samhain is a traditional Gaelic festival signifying the conclusion of the harvest season and the beginning of winter, with Celtic calendars dividing the year into two halves: Light and dark. Just as the day begins at sunrise, the New Year was thought to begin with the arrival of darkness. Samhain functioned as a new year's celebration for the Celts.

The main events of the festival were celebrated on November 1. However, initial celebrations would commence on All Hallows' Eve, October 31. Thus, this clarifies why Halloween occurs at the end of October, not on All Hallows' Day, November 1.

Samhain descends from Gaelic and Celtic tradition and was first cited in ninth-century Irish literature. However, there is a strong possibility that its history stretches back even further, as some Neolithic passage tombs dating to 4000–2500 BC align with sunrise on Samhain, indicating it was a day of high importance.

The choice of November 1 for Samhain celebrations is unlikely to be coincidental and held symbolic importance to the early Celts. As mentioned, the celebration of Samhain included the ushering in of the New Year and was seen as a time of both death and rebirth. These events happened to coincide with the end of the harvest season and the beginning of the dark and cold winter.

There is limited information on how Samhain was traditionally celebrated. Most of our sources come from legendary Celtic sagas, which explain the celebration in a more mythical manner, or Roman authors.

While the Romans kept a record of many Celtic customs, these were likely modified in their writings to act as propaganda against the Celts. Given that the Romans were constantly fighting wars against the Celts, there is some doubt among experts about how accurately they recorded cultural information and how much—if any—exaggeration existed to make the Celts look "barbaric."

This does not mean we know nothing about ancient Samhain celebrations.

There is evidence that Samhain was celebrated with grand feasts and special bonfires. People believed that the bonfires had protective and cleansing powers, and there were likely to have been rituals that involved them. It was also an event that saw the slaying of livestock and cattle taken from summer pastures.

Samhain was also considered a liminal festival—a day when the boundaries between the human world and the Otherworld were fragile. On this occasion, ancient burial mounds were unsealed due to the belief that they were portals to the Otherworld. It was also believed that Samhain was a day when the Aos Sí and other pagan gods were able to travel to the human world.

The ancient Celts would leave food and drink offerings for them to appease these gods, spirits, and fairies. Some sacrifices were symbolically burned on bonfires to act as a protective measure against mischievous and harmful spirits. The offerings were also believed to have been a way to ensure people and animals survived the harsh winter ahead.

Besides gods and the Aos Sí, spirits could also leave the Otherworld and travel to the human world on Samhain. This meant that the souls of dead relatives could visit and be welcomed by family members and loved ones. An additional plate was set at each family's table to ensure they were received with hospitality.

Harmless tricks and pranks were also common, though these were generally attributed to mischievous spirits and fairies making their way from the Otherworld. This tradition of playing pranks on Samhain can be seen in the modern tradition of children calling it "trick-or-treat" when knocking on doors. Like the spirits of Samhain, they ask for a treat that serves as protection against being pranked.

Additionally, Samhain was considered a time of looking at the future. Druids believed that the presence of spirits from the Otherworld in the human world made it easier for them to make predictions about the future, and fortune-telling rituals were a common part of Samhain celebrations.

From Samhain to Halloween

Some of the primary Samhain traditions can be seen in today's Halloween celebrations.
https://unsplash.com/photos/MYRG0ptGh50

One of the primary Samhain traditions that can be seen in today's Halloween celebrations is the practice of dressing up. During Samhain, the Celts would dress as mythical monsters and animals in the hope of confusing spirits who may wish to take them back to the Otherworld with them. The belief was that if a spirit could not identify its target, the person in question would remain unharmed until the veil between worlds was once again opaque.

This belief, of course, can be seen in the modern tradition of dressing children up as animals or mythical and fictional creatures on Halloween. However, the transition from Samhain to Halloween took centuries to accomplish.

Samhain was originally an oral tradition, with celebrations and rituals passed down from parent to child without being written down. However, this changed with the introduction of Christianity to the British Isles.

In the Middle Ages, Christian monks documented Samhain beliefs and practices, and these documents form some of the primary sources we have today that document how it was celebrated. At the same time, the Catholic Church realized that the transition from paganism to Christianity would be smoother if pagan traditions were incorporated into Christianity.

The church began a tradition of reframing these Celtic celebrations in a Christian framework, allowing them to make the most of popular pagan festivals while spreading this new religion. The best-known example of this reframing is Christmas, where the church reframed the Yule/Yuletide celebration to suit the Christian narrative.

In 609, Pope Boniface II announced a new celebration, All Saints' Day. In Middle English, this celebration was also known as All-Hallows or All-Hallowmas. In the eighth century, the date was fixed as November 1, and November 2 was declared All Souls' Day. These days were both to honor Christian martyrs.

These new festivals were celebrated in a similar way to Samhain. Bonfires were lit, and food and drink were offered, though Christians offered meals to the poor and destitute rather than to the spirits, Aos Sí, and pagan gods. Like with Samhain, celebrations would often begin before the official date of All Hallows' Day. Since celebrations would start on the evening and night of October 31, this became known as All Hallows" Eve—like the evening and night before Christmas is known as Christmas Eve.

All Hallows' Eve would, over time, evolve into Halloween, with children and adults dressing up as animals and monsters to protect them from demons that may cross the thin veil between the two worlds. Over time, this evolved into the modern secular tradition of Halloween, which remains popular even among people who do not believe in pagan or Christian origins. Instead, it has become an enjoyable evening for children to dress up and go trick-or-treating for candy.

An important part of the evolution of Samhain and All Hallows' Eve into modern Halloween was the arrival of Irish immigrants to America. When Americans learned of such traditions, they modified them, such as the example of trick-or-treating, which was initially an adults-only occasion to wear a costume and visit neighboring houses to ask for food or money.

Americans also revived some of the more traditionally pagan aspects of the celebration that had been lost following its Christianization. For example, on Halloween, young women would use yarn, mirrors, and apple parings to discover the name or appearance of their future husbands.

In the 1800s, newspapers and community leaders started working toward Halloween to become a more community- and family-based holiday. Parents were encouraged to leave anything scary or pagan out of their celebrations, which eventually led to the day not having any religious or superstitious overtones and becoming more about community.

After Halloween parties in the 1920s and 1930s led to a spate of vandalism, community leaders further moved to transform the celebration into a day for children and young adults. By the 1950s, Halloween, as we know it today, had taken shape, and a new American tradition was formed.

Other Halloween traditions also have roots in Ireland and Scotland, though not in Samhain. For example, carving pumpkins can be traced to the Scottish myth of *Stingy Jack*. The story is about a man who tricked the Devil. He was not let into either Heaven or Hell following his death through this trick. Rather, he was cursed to wander the earth with nothing but a piece of coal handed to him by the Devil.

To carry this piece of coal, Jack made a lantern out of a turnip and has roamed the earth carrying it ever since. The first Jack O'Lanterns were carved from turnips and potatoes, both easy-to-find crops in Ireland and Scotland. The ghoulish faces carved into them were done so to repel Stingy Jack and other evil spirits from the home when the veil between worlds was thin. When Irish immigrants brought the tradition to America, Jack O'Lanterns transitioned from turnips and potatoes to pumpkins, which were easier to find in this new country.

While Samhain is undoubtedly the root of modern Halloween, Halloween has evolved to be something completely different from the pagan celebration. Today's secular celebration for children bears little resemblance to the harvest festival that the ancient Celts would have celebrated. Many modern Halloween traditions have other roots, such as Scottish folklore and Christian traditions.

Samhain Then and Now

Samhain Then

As mentioned above, Samhain was a time for celebrating the harvest and the world's transition into winter. It was marked with bonfires, feasts, and rituals and was when divination was considered particularly effective.

The veil between the Otherworld and the human world was thought to be at its thinnest, so offerings were laid out to appease pagan gods and spirits that would have been able to reach the human world. People dressed as mythical monsters and animals to protect themselves from being abducted back to the Otherworld at the end of Samhain.

At the same time, there is a good chance we have lost a lot of information about the original Samhain celebrations due to a lack of primary sources. Thus, while pagans still celebrate Samhain, modern celebratory traditions have evolved to combine ancient practices and modern rituals.

Samhain Now

Modern pagans celebrate Samhain similarly to how it was celebrated in the past. There are differences, and different types of pagans also have unique celebrations.

Wiccans

Wiccans generally celebrate Samhain as part of their covens. This includes a feast for coven members and a ritual. This ritual is often public, allowing non-practicing people to experience Samhain and participate in a Wiccan ritual.

Wiccan Samhain rituals often involve honoring the dead, especially those who have died and crossed the veil since the previous year's Samhain celebration. Those who have died are named, and the four elements are called upon to help build a circle and begin the ritual. The specifics of the ritual differ from coven to coven.

Some covens observe a "dumb supper" as part of the feast. Originating in the Middle Ages, this is a tradition where the feast meal is held in silence, with a different place set at the table to honor the dead. Unlike the ritual, this is generally held privately with the coven and family members.

Wiccans who are not part of a coven also follow similar traditions, observing a personal ritual and meal, though non-practicing friends and family are often invited to the latter. Like coven rituals, the altar is central to the celebration and holds ritualistic objects, such as candles, cake, and ale.

Some Wiccan covens will also host a bonfire, generally open to the public. Non-coven Wiccans will often celebrate a bonfire with friends and family. They may also take the time to conduct divination rituals and construct a symbolic Samhain centerpiece representing the celebration, the year, and the winter ahead.

Other Wiccan Samhain traditions include telling stories of ancestors among loved ones and visiting those who had passed at the local cemetery. As it is the New Year's celebration, it is also the time to renovate at home.

Druids

As with Wiccans, Druids usually incorporate the supper into their Samhain celebrations and participate in divination rituals. Druids, in particular, saw Samhain as the ideal time to perform fortune-telling magic, and this practice continues to modern times.

Some traditional Druidic methods of divination on Samhain include:

- Pricking an egg and letting the contents drip into a glass of water, and using the shapes to tell the future.
- Using apple peelings to help young women determine the initial of the man she will marry.
- Using hazelnuts for matrimonial divination. Hazelnuts marked with the names of eligible men and women are placed in a fire in two groups (one for men, one for women). As the nuts pop, the names of those destined to be together are revealed.

Druidic celebrations of Samhain are generally relatively similar to those of Wiccans, though Druids (as mentioned above) focus more on the divinatory aspect of this day. Local Druids and Wiccans will sometimes combine celebrations and mark the day together in communities home to both a Wiccan coven and Druidic organization. One of the byproducts of this is that the celebration is generally larger and more boisterous, making it more enjoyable for everyone involved.

Other Pagan Traditions

Pagan celebrations of Samhain are relatively similar to Wiccan and Druidic traditions, given that they all draw from the same roots. However, pagan practitioners often celebrate the day individually or with close family and friends.

Some common traditions include:

- Decorating the altar.
- Participating in a private ritual.
- Making Samhain bread.

- Taking part in a Samhain nature walk to feel closer to nature. This can be done in a natural area around the practitioner's home and does not need to be an organized walk.
- Using a seven-day white candle to perform a ritual to guide the spirits to rest.
- Performing bonfire magic.
- Holding a séance.
- Performing divination magic, including through the use of runes, scrying, tarot, and other methods of divination.
- Taking the time to correct misconceptions other people may have about Samhain and working to build community connections with other pagans and non-practitioners alike.

Samhain Correspondences

Here are some Samhain correspondences that can play an important part in your day's celebration. This section will introduce these elements, and the rest of the book will go through them in detail.

The Samhain Symbol

This symbol is a looped square called a Bowen knot that joins with two inter-lapping oblong shapes, making a cross. The Bowen knot is believed to help ward off harmful spirits and bad luck, making it the perfect option for a celebration that involves appeasing the spirits and protecting oneself against the harmful attention they may bring.

Tools

- **Black and white candles.** The number you will need will depend on the rituals you are participating in—some may require small candles, while others, like the guiding ritual mentioned above, may call for larger seven-day candles.
- **Incense.** Generally handmade and incorporating the scents and elements of the season. Some ingredients to add to your incense include cinnamon, cloves, rosemary, and sage.

- **Herbs, spices, and plants.** There are many associated with Samhain, including autumn flowers like marigold and chrysanthemums, apples, mugwort, pomegranates, pumpkins and other gourds, rosemary, and rowan. Others include acorns, allspice, catnip, mountain ash, oak leaves, pine cones, sage, and straw. These can be incorporated into your celebration in many ways, including making them a part of your feast, incense, and altar, or they can be used around your home as decorations.
- **A censer for burning incense.**
- **Ritual bell.** If needed for your ritual.
- **Crystals.** Some crystals used in Samhain rituals include amethyst, labradorite, obsidian, selenite, and smoky quartz.

Animals

Animals associated with Samhain include bats, black cats, owls, ravens, and spiders. You can incorporate animal carvings of these animals in your Samhain rituals, donate to shelters and conservation organizations focused on them, or honor them in another way that works for your celebration of Samhain.

Samhain and Halloween, though often associated with each other, are, in fact, two distinctly different celebrations. Samhain has its own rich history and lore, and you will explore this lore in this book.

In the next chapter, you'll learn about the pagan deities and lore associated with Samhain and better understand its connection with death and renewal. You'll then have the chance to more deeply understand the crafts associated with the celebration and how you can decorate your home in preparation for your Samhain ritual and feast.

This book will also explain how you can set up your Samhain altar if you plan on incorporating one in your observation of this festival. If you are unsure whether it is the right option, we will cover some of the pros of having a sacred space in your home. We'll explore how to create both a seasonal and an ancestor altar and explain why the two are different.

Other parts of this book include discovering the sacred herbs and plants associated with the celebration, which you can, in turn, incorporate into your observance and feast. Additionally, we'll offer some traditional recipes you can make as part of your Samhain feast and explain why these dishes are connected to the festival.

We'll also suggest some family and group activities you can take part in as part of your celebrations, allowing you to allow non-practicing loved ones to get a better understanding of this important day. We'll additionally cover the rituals and ceremonies that you can use in your Samhain celebrations, including kid-friendly variations when practicing with your children.

Finally, you'll learn about spells, charms, and baths that are highly potent when worked on and around Samhain, including love magic, abundance charms, divination magic, and protection spells. We'll also cover some prayers and blessings you can read during your Samhain observance and meditation. This will include prayers and blessings for Wiccans, Druids, and pagans, so you'll know how to incorporate the traditions of your loved ones and friends into your own celebration of the day.

By the time you have read this book, all your questions about Samhain will have been answered. All you need to do is turn this page and keep reading!

Chapter 2: Samhain Deities and Lore

This chapter will discuss the gods and goddesses related to Samhain. Since Samhain is connected to death, the deities connected to this holiday will also be associated with death and the underworld. So, let us dive into this chapter, and you can learn everything about the deities of Samhain.

The Crone

Firstly, we will discuss the Crone, who is one-third of the triple Goddess and made up of the Mother, Maiden, and Crone. The Crone represents death and wisdom and is the guardian of the underworld. The Crone is most powerful during Samhain. She goes by many names since every culture has its own Crone. The ancient Greeks called her "Hecate," the Welsh's Crone was "Cerridwen," and the Scottish and Irish Celtic Crone was "Cailleach."

Hecate

Hecate is the Greek Crone. She is the goddess of ghosts, crossroads, magic, the moon, necromancy, the night, and witchcraft. She was the daughter of the Titan Perses and the nymph Asteria, both minor deities. Hecate was associated with the dead, ghosts, and the spiritual world, explaining her connection to Samhain. In various depictions, Hecate was portrayed holding a key that was believed to be the key to the underworld or two torches to guide the spirits of the dead. She was very powerful. In fact, Zeus gave her power over the sea, earth, and heaven. Hecate was also known for her healing powers and vast knowledge.

There is not much known about Hecate. This may be because this goddess loved to remain mysterious, while some believe historians were afraid to utter her name. The best time to call on Hecate is on October 31, the night of Samhain. This is because it is the day when the veil between the physical world and the spiritual world is at its thinnest.

Hecate can take the form of the Triple Goddess and can easily travel from the underworld to the physical world.

Persephone

The gods and goddesses of the underworld can speak to us on Samhain, but the loudest voice of them all is that of the goddess Persephone. She was the queen of the underworld since she was married to Hades. She was the daughter of Demeter, goddess of fertility and agriculture, and Zeus, the god of the sky and the chief deity. As well as being the queen of the underworld, Persephone was also the goddess of fertility, just like her mother. She was a very attractive girl with many gods who fell in love with her, but her mother was obsessed with her daughter and would not allow any of these gods to come near her. Hades wanted to marry her, but Demeter refused, so he kidnapped Persephone and married her, and this was how she became the queen of the underworld.

Naturally, Demeter was not pleased that her daughter had been taken from her. Zeus interfered, and they reached a compromise. Persephone would spend one-third of the year in the underworld with Hades and two-thirds with her mother, Demeter. Persephone spent all autumn and winter in the underworld, and it is believed that she ascended her throne in the underworld during Samhain. As the queen of the underworld, Persephone also became the goddess of death. She was initially called "Core," which means "the maiden," when she was only the goddess of spring and before marrying Hades and becoming the queen of the underworld.

However, in various ancient texts, instead of her real name, Core, the goddess is referred to as Persephone, a name which means "the bringer of death"—ever since she became the ruler of the underworld after marrying Hades. Although the name may imply something negative, Persephone was portrayed positively in many myths. The goddess helped mortals and provided them with wisdom, making her the goddess of rebirth. Death and rebirth are regarded as strong themes for Samhain, as many people associate the gods of the living and the dead with this day. Persephone had another connection with Samhain as she controlled the gates between the worlds of the living and the dead. These gates are responsible for thinning the veil between both worlds, especially during Samhain.

Cerridwen

If you wonder why the image of the cauldron is usually associated with Samhain festivities, it is because of the Goddess Cerridwen. Cerridwen was a very powerful Celtic goddess who lived in the underworld. She was the goddess of mystery, transformation, magic, inspiration, enchantment, regeneration, knowledge, and death. Cerridwen had a magical, powerful cauldron containing a potion, and whoever drank it would get immense knowledge. Cerridwen was the Welsh's Crone and represented the darker side of the Triple Goddess.

She had two children, a beautiful girl called Crearwy and a hideous boy named Afagddu. Cerridwen wanted to give her son an advantage, so she created a potion to grant him knowledge and wisdom. The potion required brewing for a whole year and a day. The goddess made her servant Gwion responsible for the brew until it reached full potency. However, three drops splashed out and scalded his thumb while stirring the potion. Without thinking, he put his thumb in his mouth and, in turn, consumed the potion droplets. Gwion was then gifted with all the knowledge and wisdom Cerridwen wanted to give her son.

Gwion escaped out of fear, with Cerridwen chasing after him. Each of them would transform into a different creature during the chase until she managed to catch him and consume him. She then became pregnant and knew the child was her servant who had been reborn. This chase has become a symbol of transformation, rebirth, and death, which are themes associated with Samhain.

Cerridwen is one of the goddesses strongly associated with Samhain. As a representative of the Triple Goddess's dark side and as a goddess of the underworld, Cerridwen visits her worshippers during the time of Samhain as the world transforms from light into darkness (the end of summer and the beginning of fall).

Cerridwen uses her cauldron to help transform us as well by helping us place our bad habits and negative thoughts into the pot. Since Cerridwen is associated with Samhain and the cauldron is a symbol associated with her, it has also become a symbol for the festival. The cauldron represents transformation, magic, mystery, and inspiration, which are all themes associated with Samhain, a time of mystery and magic.

Fun Fact: It is believed that Cerridwen's cauldron is the Holy Grail mentioned in the Arthurian legends.

The Morrigan

The Morrigan is the goddess of war and could predict who would die during a battle. She could transform into a crow and fly over the battle. She served as an inspiration to the soldiers so that they kept fighting and instilled fear into the hearts of their opponents. The Morrigan's association with Samhain resulted from her role in the battle of the Plain of Pillar (Cathe Maige Tuired), which took place during Samhain. The battle was between the Tuatha Dé Danann (a supernatural race of deities in ancient Ireland) and the Fomorians (a hostile supernatural race in Irish mythology). She met with the chief god of the Tuatha Dé Danann, Dagda, around the time of Samhain and gave him the advice to help him in the battle. The battle began on Samhain when the Morrigan appeared to the Tuatha Dé Danann soldiers to motivate them to keep fighting so they could defeat their opponents.

The Morrigan's assistance worked as the Tuatha Dé Danann defeated the Fomorians. She also played a crucial role in the battle of Cattle Raid of Cooley (Táin Bó Cuiligne), which also took place during Samhain. Similar to her role in the battle of the Plain of Pillar, the Morrigan also inspired the soldiers of this battle to fight to win the war. As a goddess prophesied death and played two major roles in battles on Samhain, we can easily see how she is now associated with this day. In fact, some pagans choose to celebrate the Morrigan during the festival due to her connection to Samhain and because she does not have another day associated with her.

Hel

Hel is the Norse goddess of death and the queen of the afterlife. Her father is Loki, the god of mischief, and her mother is the giantess Angrboda. Although she is often called a goddess, Hel is considered a half goddess since her mother was not a deity. She was abducted along with her brothers and was sent to the underworld. She was responsible for the souls of the dishonored dead. Hel can also release the spirits of the dead back to the physical world. When her father Loki killed her uncle Baldr, the god of courage and wisdom, Odin was distraught, so his other son Hermóðr, the messenger of the gods, decided to ride to the kingdom of the dead to bring his brother back. Hel agreed to send Baldr back, provided that all living and dead creatures would weep for him. As the goddess of death and ruler of the underworld who can release the souls of the dead, Hel can be connected to Samhain.

Cailleach

Cailleach, as mentioned earlier, is the Scottish and Irish crone. She is the goddess of winter, sorcery, and diseases. She can also control the weather. Her season begins on Samhain, October 31, and ends on May 1 or Beltane. She represents the death that takes place during the winter and the rebirth that occurs during the spring.

Anubis

Now we shall discuss male deities, starting with the Egyptian god Annubis. You are probably wondering how an Egyptian god is connected to Samhain. Since he is the god of death in ancient Egyptian culture, his association with this festival makes sense. He was also the god of the afterlife, mummification, the underworld, and tombs. Anubis is his Greek name, while his Egyptian name is Anpu which means "to decay."

You will not find a holiday similar to Samhain in ancient or modern Egypt. However, the ancient Egyptian religion was filled with themes about death, the spirits of the dead, the afterlife, and many other similar themes. Even the pyramids were built around the idea of death and the afterlife.

Anubis is also considered a guardian and protector. He resided between the underworld and the earth to help guide the spirits of the dead to the afterlife. Annubis is also associated with the Sirius star, which connects him to the mysteries of the astral realm. Since Samhain is a time associated with the spirits of the dead and mystery and secrets, naturally, Annubis, the god of death and the master of secrets (Hery Sesheta) and keeper of the mysteries of the universe, is connected to this day.

Osiris

Osiris is another Egyptian deity and a god of the underworld. He was one of the most important gods in Egyptian mythology. He was married to his sister, Isis, the goddess of death, rebirth, and magic. According to certain legends and myths, Osiris and Annubis were related. Some legends say that Osiris was Annubis's nephew, while others say they were father and son. Although they were both connected to death, both gods played different roles. As mentioned, Annubus helped guide the spirits of the dead to the underworld, while Osiris ruled over the underworld and judged the souls.

Before ruling over the underworld, Osiris ruled over Egypt. He had a brother called Seth, who was consumed with anger and jealousy toward Osiris. Seth killed Osiris, cut his body into pieces, and scattered them all over Egypt. Seth then ruled Egypt with his wife, Nephthys (his sister). Isis, Osiris's wife, and Seth and Nephthys's sister were heartbroken over her husband's death and wept for him every day. Nephthys took pity on her sister, and both decided to find Osiris's parts to bring him back to life. Annubis also played a role by inventing embalming—a process to protect the body from decay—until Thoth, the Egyptian god of the moon, taught Isis the magical rituals necessary to resurrect her husband. When Osiris came back to life, Isis conceived a child with him named Horus, who became the god of the sky. Osiris did not stay long in the world of the living and went to rule the underworld.

So how is all of this connected to Samhain? Isis collected Osiris's parts during Samhain from October 28 to November 2, and he was resurrected on November 3. Samhain is also considered the pagan new year, a time of rebirth and resurrection. This meant that Osiris, Isis, Anubis, Toth, and Nephthys were all associated with Samhain.

Cernunnos

Now we will go back to the Celtic gods with Cernunnos, the horned god of the forest. He was associated with vegetation, fertility, and male animals. According to Neo-Wiccan traditions, Cernunnos died during the fall, which affected vegetation during this time of year. However, he was resurrected in the spring and impregnated by the fertile goddess of the land.

Unfortunately, there is not much known about Cernunnos. However, his associations with the themes of death and resurrection and many of his images that depict his association with the underworld create an association between Cernunnos and Samhain. Some Wiccans seek the help of Cernunnos when they want to open the portal between our world and the world of the dead.

Dionysus

Dionysus is the Greek god of wine, mirth, and fertility. So how is the god of wine connected to Samhain? Well, Dionysus is associated with death as a result of his legend. He was the son of Zeus and a mortal woman named Semele, who Zeus was madly in love with. Semele knew her lover was a god, but she had no idea he was the chief deity, Zeus. Hera learned about her husband's infidelity and went to Semele to convince her to ask Zeus to show her his true form. When Zeus visited his lover, she made this request and made him swear he would oblige. Zeus could not break his oath and couldn't refuse his lover's request. Once he appeared in his real form, Semele burnt to ashes since no mortal could handle the sight of such a glorious god. Semele was pregnant at the time, so Zeus rescued his unborn child by stitching the fetus into his thigh until he was born.

When Dionysus was born, Hera was still consumed with jealousy over her husband's betrayal and sent Titans to kill the little boy. They succeeded and ripped his body apart. However, Rhea, Zeus's mother and the goddess of fertility and motherhood, resurrected her grandson. Dionysus was one of the few gods who could travel to the underworld and bring a dead person back. Although he never met his mother, she was always on his mind. One day, he decided to travel to the underworld and bring her back to the world of the living, and he succeeded. Since he is associated with death, resurrection, and the underworld, Dionysus is another god connected to Samhain's festivities.

Arawn

Arawn is a god closely associated with the Druids. He is the Celtic god of death and revenge and ruled over the underworld. He is depicted as a tall man wearing a gray cloak with an intimidating appearance. However, Arawn's kingdom was known to be a very peaceful place. He was also an honorable and fair ruler but showed a ruthless side to wrongdoers. The god of death is also associated with the decay that usually occurs during the winter and the fall. It is a time of death and transformation, themes that both Arawn and Samhain shared.

Arawn guarded the spirits of the dead and watched over the underworld to ensure no spirit escaped to the realm of the living. However, every year he makes an exception that takes place on the night of Samhain when the veil between the world of the living and the dead is at its thinnest, and the portal of the underworld is opened, allowing the spirits of the dead to enter the realm of the living.

Hades

We cannot talk about gods of death and the underworld without mentioning Hades, the Greek god of the dead and ruler of the underworld, and Zeus's brother. As mentioned earlier, Hades lived in the underworld and only left it to kidnap Persephone. His name means "the unseen one," which was appropriate for a god who ruled over a world that was "unseen" to the living. As the god of death and the ruler of the underworld, Hades was feared by many. However, he was not an evil god as he is often represented. In fact, Hades was extremely selfless, a quality that not many ancient Greeks were aware of. He only cared about his realm and defending the rights of the spirits of the dead. However, Hades would get very angry whenever anyone tried to steal souls from his realm and bring them back to the world of the living. His punishment could be ruthless. Since Hades mainly resided in the underworld, he is not featured in many legends, but his connection to the dead and the underworld accounts for his association with Samhain.

Pluto

Pluto is the god of death and the ruler of the underworld in Roman mythology. He shares many similarities with his Greek counterpart, Hades. He resided in the underworld and showed no interest in the world of the living. Nor did he interfere with the matters of the gods. Just like Hades, Pluto also abducted the goddess of fertility, but in Roman mythology, she was called Prosperina. Similar to how Hades was associated with Samhain, Pluto is also connected to this day as the Roman god of death and ruler of the underworld.

Mictlāntēcuhtli

Mictlāntēcuhtli is the Aztec god of death and ruler of the Aztec underworld, similar to his Greek and Roman counterparts, Hades and Pluto. Unlike Greek and Roman gods, Mictlāntēcuhtli was not the son of another deity. He was created by Huitzilopochtli (the god of war), Tezcatlipoca (creator deity), Quetzalcoatl (the god of wind), and Xipe Totact (the god of agriculture and the seasons) when they were building the universe. However, unlike his counterparts, Mictlāntēcuhtli did not need to kidnap his wife, Mictēcacihuatl. She was created simultaneously with her husband, and they both ruled the underworld together.

As the ruler of the underworld and the god of death, Mictlāntēcuhtli is also associated with the night of Samhain. Mictlāntēcuhtli focused on his domain and only wanted to establish order in the land of the dead. According to the Aztecs, all the spirits of the dead had to face Mictlāntēcuhtli. There was no heaven or hell—or any equivalent of a good or bad place after death—and all spirits shared the same fate. However, according to other myths, the Aztecs believed in various forms of paradise. Those who didn't get to paradise would travel to the underworld and suffer at the hands of Mictlāntēcuhtli, who enjoyed torturing them. For this reason, he is often portrayed as an evil god. However, he still had good character since he would sometimes grant life.

Hermes

According to Greek mythology, Hermes is the messenger of the gods and the god of flocks, roads, thieves, and commerce. He is associated with the underworld since he helped the spirits of the dead and provided them with guidance. Hermes was connected to the goddess Hecate since they could easily travel between worlds. As a result of this connection, just like Hecate, Hermes is also honored during the festivities of Samhain. Of all the Olympian gods, Hermes was the only one to travel between the living and the dead realms and delivered the spirits of the dead to Hades in the underworld.

Samhain is when the spirits of the dead can travel from the underworld to visit our physical world. Naturally, all the gods associated with this day are gods of death, the underworld, and resurrection.

Chapter 3: Samhain Crafts and Decorations

How you decorate your home for Samhain can reveal your spiritual beliefs and passion for this special time of year. Ominous rites and traditions mark Samhain, and the occasion would certainly be incomplete without eerie décor. Using Samhain crafts to decorate your home will help create the ideal ambiance for the sacred occasion. Here are some simple Samhain crafts and decorations ideas to inspire you on how to decorate your house for Samhain.

Samhain vs. Halloween Decorations

Halloween and Samhain share a common history and are celebrated on the same date. However, there is a contrasting difference between the two. While Halloween is simply a spooky holiday, Samhain is a unique spiritual experience. Samhain is a day for honoring the dead and is a serious occasion in Celtic paganism. When darkness falls on Samhain, the veil between the living and the dead is at its thinnest. Spirits are considered to visit the land of the living, and thus, the decor adorning your house should be inviting to certain spirits while warding off evil ones.

Color Scheme and Symbols

Samhain is the last harvest season out of the three celebrated in Celtic tradition, and thus, a harvest theme should be followed when decorating for this occasion. The color palette you should adopt includes warm fall shades like orange, maroon, red, and mustard. Other tones include dark pink and dark purple.

Proper decor should also include symbols, sigils, runes, and crystals that depict the Samhain tradition and values. These can include:

Symbols

The symbol for Samhain is the Bowen knot, represented by a looped square and two oblong shapes that form a cross. The Bowen knot is a symbol of protection to ward off evil spirits. Considering the spooky time of Samhain, this symbol is often displayed on front doors and windows to repel any evil spirits or negative energies.

Runes

There are several runes you can carve or inscribe into various decoration items. Each of these has a specific meaning. Important runes for Samhain include:

- *Eihwaz* — Invites the spirits from their realm.
- *Perthro* — Symbolizes sanctuary for the spirits.
- *Kano* — To brighten the way for the spirits.
- *Elhaz* — Protects against evil spirits.

Crystals

Amethyst.
https://unsplash.com/photos/ToDanUwG4vs?utm_source=unsplash&utm_medium=referral&utm_content=creditShareLink

Samhain crystals can be used to honor the beginning of darkness and death. They can be used as decorations or in Samhain rituals. Important crystals for Samhain include:

- *Obsidian* — A pitch-black crystal with protective energy to help ward off evil spirits and repel negative energies.
- *Labradorite* — A shiny blue-gray crystal that can be used to help communicate with the spirits as they cross over into the realm of the living.
- *Amethyst* — A unique violet-colored crystal that is said to form a protective bubble around its owner to ward off evil spirits.
- *Smoky Quartz* — This crystal can help draw spirits close to you and facilitate conversation between you.
- *Selenite* — A white crystal with high-frequency energy is ideal for achieving mental clarity.

Ancestor Altar Cloth

Many people tend to practice ancestor-focused rituals during Samhain, and there is nothing better than using an ancestor altar cloth for this. The altar cloth can also be used to decorate your house and give off a spiritual Samhain vibe. This is easy to make and requires little effort.

Materials Needed:

- An unpatterned white piece of fabric
- Fabric markers or embroidery cotton
- A fabric pencil
- Your ancestral genealogy

Instructions:

1. Using a thread and needle, embroider the names into the cloth or write down the genealogy chart with a fabric marker.
2. Start by writing your name in the middle using a lightweight fabric pencil. Add your date and place of birth as well. Make sure you distribute the space to fit the names in evenly.
3. Branch out and add the names of your parents, your spouse's parents, and their grandparents and move as far up the ancestral line as you can.
4. You can use Post-it notes to place the names on the cloth first to ensure you do not make any mistakes. Once you have done this, either embroider the names or write them down using fabric markers.
5. In the end, you can add pictures of yourself, your parents, grandparents, and ancestors if you have any you wish to add.

Grave Rubbing

Pagan culture considers death not an ending but the beginning of a new journey. This is why grave rubbings are pretty common during Samhain. While most people use their relative's or ancestors' headstones, there are no limits, and you can use any headstone you find striking. However, be very careful when doing grave rubbing, as it can be destructive for headstones if done incorrectly.

Materials Needed:

- Lightweight paper
- A large dark-colored crayon
- Rubbing wax
- Masking tape
- A paintbrush
- A cardboard tube (optional)

Instructions:

1. Use the paintbrush to wipe dust and debris off the grave's headstone.
2. Place the paper over the area you want to trace, and use masking tape to secure it over the headstone.
3. Try to cover the rest of the headstone to avoid getting crayon marks on the stone.
4. Use the crayon to start filling the outer edges of the carved area. Then, move to the center and shade outward toward the edges until the complete headstone is covered.
5. Step back and observe your rubbing. If there is any color variation, add more definition to that region.
6. Carefully remove the masking tape and place it in the cardboard tube, so you do not damage it.
7. Frame the rubbing when you get home and hang it near the Samhain altar.

Bowls and Baskets Galore

What better way to follow the Samhain theme than by displaying a variety of traditional food? Traditional Samhain food dishes are discussed in a later chapter, but some food items can also be used as decor items.

Materials Needed:

- Bowls and baskets from a thrift store
- Harvest season foods, e.g., corn, apples, small pumpkins, etc.
- Autumn leaves

Instructions:

1. Take a basket and fill it with seasonal fruit and vegetables, including pumpkins, apples, red grapes, cabbage, etc.
2. Place these baskets on tables and counters all around your house.
3. Place the autumn leaves beside and under these baskets to create a seasonal atmosphere.

Pumpkin Carvings

Ancient Celts used to carve scary faces into turnips and other vegetables to ward off evil spirits during Samhain. While times have changed, and so have many traditions during Samhain, carving up a pumpkin is still one of the most practiced traditions for Pagans and Wiccans. Carved pumpkins adorned with Samhain symbols and runes make the perfect decoration for this time of the year.

Materials Needed:

- 1 pumpkin
- A small food knife
- A scooping spoon
- A sharpie
- A small container

Instructions:
1. Thoroughly wash your pumpkin and wipe it down to dry it and remove any dust particles.
2. While you can try to draw Samhain symbols and inscriptions by hand, a much easier way is to download Samhain stencils and secure them over the pumpkin with masking tape to draw flawless symbols or even scary faces.
3. Once you have traced the design on the pumpkin, it is time to start carving. Keep a big container close to you to dump the pumpkin fillings in.
4. Use the food knife to cut a circular lid around the pumpkin's stem and pull it out. Start removing the pumpkin seeds, and put them aside.
5. Use the scooping spoon to remove all the pumpkin fillings and throw them away. Make sure you remove as much material as you can.
6. Once you've finished removing your pumpkin's innards, rinse it thoroughly to get rid of all the stickiness.
7. Using the same food knife, start carving the design you traced earlier from the stencils. Do not worry about being neat right now; simply make the carvings.
8. Now, use a craft knife to neaten the edges. Once you have finished carving, place a candle inside the pumpkin and set the lid back on top.

Crystal Balls and Candles

Crystal balls are the perfect Samhain decor items, with their witchy feel and ornate designs. Plus, there are a ton of crystal balls available at affordable prices, with so many features. Some crystal balls have built-in light and blurred glass designs to create an eerie vibe. Candles are also a cliché Samhain decoration, without which the festivities would be incomplete. Black candles are particularly suitable during Samhain festivals and can be placed all around the house for a dark, spooky vibe.

Skeleton Decor

Samhain is a festival for the dead, where we celebrate our ancestors and honor their spirits. What better decorations could you use than skeletons and bones around your house? There are many options for creating skeleton and bone decor pieces for Samhain. Skulls are common items for Samhain, bringing a spooky vibe to the room. So, here are some ideas for skeleton decor for Samhain.

1. Take a regular old skull decoration and spray-paint it black. Connect some butterfly decor pieces to the skull.
2. Take small-sized skull decor pieces, place them on a stand, and put a transparent dome on top.
3. Take a few skull decor pieces and tie them together with a rope. Alternate their colors and hang them outside your front door.
4. Spray paint a regular skull piece golden and decorate it with some vibrant flowers to catch attention.
5. Take the upper part of a skull and adorn it with sequins and rhinestones for a sparkly look. Place a large pearl piece in the eye socket for an even more creative look.
6. Place a few skulls and bones on your dinner table and combine them with long white candles for an eerie, Victorian look.

Corn Dolls

Corn dolls have been a part of the pagan culture for centuries, where they were used in various rituals. According to old witch traditions, corn dollies bring their owners health, wealth, and luck. Today, they are still a part of Samhain traditions and make the perfect spooky decorations for this festival. They can also later be used in different rituals during Samhain.

Materials Needed:

- A bowl of water
- Corn husks
- Glue
- Old fabric

- Paints or markers
- Scissors
- String

Instructions:
1. Place the corn husks in the bowl and soak them until they are soft.
2. Using a piece of string, take a few husks and bind them together.
3. Keep the bunch in one hand for the head and fold the husks downward.
4. To make a face, level out the husks and use another piece of string to tie them around the neck.
5. For the arms, roll up one piece of husk and tighten it with a string from both ends.
6. Bring both arms together in the front and bind them with more string.
7. Use another piece of string to tie in the middle and form the waist.
8. To make the legs, divide the husks into two sections, and bind them at the knees and ankles.
9. To add accessories and clothes, use fabric to design the clothes or hats for the doll. Use the markers to draw on a face for the dolly.

Garlands

While you can easily find Garlands matching the Samhain vibe you are trying to create. There is nothing better than DIY-ing crafts for holidays like these. Plus, garlands can be hung in any room or even outdoors and are quite easy to make. This easy-to-make garland will have three different shapes: Spider, pumpkin, and ghost, each portraying a Samhain symbol.

Materials Needed:
- Twine
- Scissors

- Orange, black, and white yarn
- 1 dining chair
- Green and black pipe cleaners

Instructions:
1. To make the spider, wrap the black yarn around the upper part of the dining chair. The more yarn you wrap, the thicker your shape will be.
2. Wind the black yarn about 75 times around the chair and then slide it off. Tie three loops around the yarn in a perpendicular direction to the yarns.
3. Now, equally cut three portions of the yarn bundle between the middle two loops. Trim the yarn from both sides, so it looks like a spider.
4. Take two black pipe cleaners for the spider's legs and cut them in half. Attach these pipe cleaners to the spider's body with some glue. Use the loop thread to hang the spiders.
5. Wrap the orange yarn around the chair for the pumpkin and slide it off.
6. Cut the yarn into three pieces as you did with the spider. Trim the pumpkin, and add a stem using the pipe cleaners.
7. Simply bend the cleaners around the tied loop and connect them with yarn to hang the pumpkin.
8. Finally, to make the ghost, wrap the white yarn around the chair, slide it off, and cut it from one end, so you get a long bunch of yarn.
9. Tie one piece of the yarn in the center to get two separate portions of the yarn. Fold the two portions together and tie another yarn toward the upper end to create the head of the ghost.
10. Hang these shapes using the twine and set it over the fireplace or anywhere else you would like—be careful that it does not create a fire hazard.

Luminaries

Luminaries can be used to decorate walkways and staircases with brilliantly illuminating pieces that will create a mystical look in your house. You can make luminaries of all shapes and sizes and place them around your house, on staircases, and even outdoors. Plus, this craft is one of the easiest to make and does not require many supplies.

Materials Needed:

- White paper sheets
- Crayons, markers, and colored pencils
- Tape
- Tea lights (battery operated)
- Glass jars
- A sharpie

Instructions:

1. Get printable stencils to draw different scary faces, Samhain symbols, runes, and sigils.
2. Tape the stencils to the white sheets and trace the patterns with a sharpie, markers, crayons, or colored pencils.
3. Once you have done that, remove the stencils carefully without spreading the color.
4. Fold the sheet in a circular shape, with the patterns on the outer side of the sheet, and use tape to enclose the sheet.
5. Place the tea lights inside a glass jaw and turn them on.
6. Place the luminary on top of the jar to enclose the whole thing; the sheet starts glowing.

While Samhain used to be a spooky and eerie season for the ancient Celts and pagans, it is now celebrated with full fervor to honor the dead. Although Samhain is considered different from Halloween, the decor for both holidays comprises spooky items and ornamentations. However, Samhain consists of much more eerie adornments that portray the beliefs behind Samhain. As a modern witch, these decor ideas will assist you when looking for ways to decorate your home for Samhain.

Chapter 4: Setting Up Your Samhain Altar

As previously discussed, one of the ways for Wiccans and pagans to celebrate Samhain is by decorating their altar and using it in a Samhain ritual. If you have never had an altar at your house, you may wonder how to make and use one. Other common questions about altars include whether there are different types and the benefits of having one in your home.

If you've asked yourself any of these questions, this is the chapter for you. By the time you've moved on, you will know all there is to know about setting up your Samhain altar.

Benefits of Setting Up an Altar

An altar is a sacred place in your home that you can use when performing rituals. Altars have been associated with and used for divine practices for millennia. Each tradition has variations on an altar and how it is used, from Catholicism to Buddhism to pagan religions.

The altar essentially serves as an outward representation of your inner spirituality. It is a place that helps honor your ideas and beliefs and serves as a calming space in your home that you can go to when you want to connect with yourself or your gods.

While an altar is often considered a formal space for worship and ritual, many practitioners find it a place where they can pause, reflect, and center themselves. It acts as a space that provides a sense of comfort and calm and a place where you can stay connected to your spiritual side.

An altar at home is a good place to start nourishing the part of yourself that needs more self-care due to a gap in your spirituality. It can also serve as a reminder to be less harsh and more mindful of yourself and your needs and to take time to meet your self-care needs.

An altar also serves as a focal point for your spirituality. It allows you a space where you can focus while praying, meditating, or simply practicing breath work and gratitude. It allows you to connect with the deities you worship more deeply. You may even find that an altar makes it easier to develop pre-existing rituals into personalized ones tailored for you and your needs.

Types of Altars

There are numerous types of altars you can build. Most are personalized to you and your practice. However, there are two major categories that most altars fall under: Ancestor altars and seasonal altars.

Ancestor Altars

An ancestor altar is pretty much what it sounds like—a way for you to honor the people who came before you and helped shape who you are today, and this is a popular option on Samhain. After all, Samhain is a time to honor the dead, and an ancestor altar is one of the ways to do so.

An ancestor altar can be as big as you want. You can use a full table for it or just the corner of a shelf. The size does not matter, only your intent. Though called an "ancestor" altar, it is a way to honor all those who have gone before you, whether they are pets or cherished friends.

Seasonal Altars

Like ancestor altars, a seasonal altar is almost exactly what it says in the name—an altar you set up and change as the seasons change. It is a way for you to honor the cycle of the seasons and help you feel more in touch with nature. It can also be a focal point when working seasonal magic or celebrating the Sabbats.

These altars are generally made by incorporating parts or symbols of the season into your altar. For example, you would honor new life and rebirth for a spring altar and incorporate elements such as fresh flowers and images of maiden goddesses on the altar. Similarly, the space will change and evolve as the seasons do, ensuring you keep connected to nature.

Creating an Altar

When creating an altar, first make space for it in your home. As mentioned, this space does not have to be big, especially if you do not have much space to spare—but you should first create a dedicated place where you can build your altar without it being intruded upon by other parts of your life.

Ideally, the space should be a flat or raised surface. When creating an altar, first create protective boundaries around it. If possible, ensure the altar is in a quiet, out-of-the-way space in your home that does not see much traffic. After all, you don't want it to get knocked over or damaged by mistake.

Additionally, be very aware of your emotions. Does the space you are choosing feel "right?" Is it quiet and peaceful? Do you think you will be able to practice and perform rituals in this space? Does the energy feel bright and happy? Though you may not be able to categorize it empirically, you'll likely be able to tell if a space is right for your altar or not.

Keep in mind that you can have more than one altar in your home. You can even create an altar in your garden if that feels like it is the best location on your property. There are no hard-and-fast rules on where the altars should be located, aside from ensuring that it's the right spot for you and your needs.

Once you have chosen a space, clear it of any debris and clutter, and make sure it will remain that way.

Ancestor Altars

The first step toward creating an ancestor altar is physically cleaning the chosen altar of dirt and debris. You would not invite a loved one to sit in a dirty chair, and you should not invite them to use a dirty space as an altar.

Consider consecrating the area or smudging it with sage or sweetgrass to help make it feel welcoming. You can also sprinkle some consecrated water or consecrate it with the four elements. You will need a white candle, water, salt, and incense to do so. Each item links to a cardinal direction and an element:

Candle = fire/South

Water = water/West

Salt = earth/North

Incense = fire/East.

Light the candle and incense, and pass each item over the altar, facing the related cardinal direction. Speak or chant, asking the element and direction to consecrate your altar. Once you have done this for all four, finish by asking the sky and the spirits to do so.

Add an altar cloth to help welcome the ancestors. Depending on your practice and spiritual traditions, this cloth may need to be very specific or could be anything at all. For example, some practitioners believe that a red cloth should be used, while others require the cloth to have a fringe. Use a neat cloth that corresponds to your beliefs.

Welcome the ancestors to your altar by choosing photographs of them that have some meaning to you. If you do not have photos, use an item that may have belonged to them or an item representing who they were. You can also use symbols representing those that came before—for example, if you have a family crest, you can add that to your altar to symbolically represent all your family members who have passed.

Once you've added items representing the people you want to honor, add other items you can use in your practice when honoring your ancestors. These will differ based on what you use, but some options include votive candles, a symbol of your spirituality (like a pentagram or an ankh), and a cauldron or cup to symbolize the

Earth Mother.

You can also leave food offerings on the altar so that the spirits can share your meal with you. Some people leave portions of their meal, while others leave representations of a meal—either as ingredients, like wheat or herbs, or through representational items like bread made of plastic or metal. What you choose will depend on your personal beliefs.

Taking care of your ancestor altar is relatively stress-free. Make sure it is well maintained and clean at all times. If you leave food offerings, make sure to respectfully dispose of them before they go bad. You can do this by ritually burning or burying them, feeding them to the local wild animals, or eating them yourself.

Your choice will largely depend on your personal beliefs and which option works best for you. For example, someone in a city may find burying food offerings or feeding them to wild animals impractical, and others may believe consuming an offering to the spirits is disrespectful. Choose the method that works best for you and your practice.

If you feel like the energy around your ancestor altar is dulling or stagnant, feel free to move it to a new location. And if you have more space than expected, consider expanding the altar if possible.

While your ancestor altar will come in useful on Samhain, when the veil between the worlds is at its thinnest, you can also use it to honor your loved ones on their birthdays and on other days that were significant to them, such as a special anniversary the two of you shared.

Seasonal Altar

Getting started with your seasonal altar is similar to how you start building your ancestor altar. Clear the area you will be using and consecrate it. Once you have done so, you can start filling the area.

For Samhain, you will be building a fallen altar. While Samhain signifies the start of winter, winter has not yet started when celebrating this day.

Some items you can add to your altar include representations of the waning moon—the moon phase associated with this season and seasonally associated with fall. You can also add herbs, spices, and plants associated with the season, such as marigold flowers, acorns, sage, sweetgrass, and cedar.

You should also add crystals associated with fall, such as hematite and indigo gabbro. Other common additions include leaves that have naturally fallen from trees as the season changes, black candles, and tarot cards linked to the fall, such as the Death card and the Queen of Wands. Some practitioners may also add a Rudraksha seed mala, but this differs based on your beliefs.

Fall is a time to release and let go, so you can also add items representing things, ideas, and people you want to let go of this fall. Finally, you can add images of crone goddesses you believe in, such as Hecate, Baba Yaga, or Elli.

Taking care of your fall altar is similar to how you would take care of your ancestor altar—ensure the area is clean and well maintained, and respectfully dispose of food and other items that may start to decompose if left out. Once fall is over, remove the items that make up your fall altar, clear the space, and re-consecrate before building your winter altar.

Samhain Altar

While you can use your seasonal fall altar for Samhain rituals, building a separate altar dedicated to Samhain for the big day is also possible. Samhain is a celebration of the fall, the harvest season, and the circle of life and death; your altar will represent this.

First, clean and consecrate the area that will be used. Then, start to build the altar. Cover the altar with a cloth (or cloths) representing the season's colors, such as black, deep reds, rich purples, or harvest colors like orange and gold.

The candles you add to your altar should also represent these darker shades. Alternatively, add candles of contrasting colors like white or silver, especially if you use them in rituals.

Samhain is a time to celebrate and honor the dead and the dying of the crops and life so that the cycle of life can start anew. Add symbols of death to your altars, such as skulls, scythes, ghosts, skeletons, or grave rubbings. If you are not setting up a separate ancestor shrine, you can add items representing loved ones, such as the ashes of those who have passed.

Other additions to your Samhain altar should be other symbols of the celebration, such as mulled wine, fallen leaves and acorns, a straw man, dark bread and/or ears of corn and wheat, and similar items. If you do not have a separate ancestor altar, add offerings to the spirits. Add images or statues of deities representing death, such as Hades, depending on your religious beliefs.

Given that Samhain is a harvest festival, you should also add some of the year's last harvest products. If you have a home garden, include some herbs and fruit you have grown yourself. If you live in an agricultural area, opt for local products from a nearby farmer's market. If not, add some apples, pumpkin, squash, and other fruits and vegetables that symbolize the harvest. You can also add some harvest and farming tools, like sickles.

Finally, add any divination tools you may use on Samhain. Samhain is the time when divination magic is widespread and easier to perform, thanks to the thin veil between worlds. Thus, additional tools such as tarot cards, a pendulum, a scrying mirror, and any other tools you will use for this task can be added. These tools should ideally be re-consecrated before you add them to your altar and use them in divination magic.

Once you have your altar (or altars) ready for Samhain, the next step is to use it. As mentioned above, your altar can serve as a focal point for your practice. It is also a good way to honor the spirits and those who have gone before you. However, if you are drawn to ritual and magic, you can use the altar for these purposes.

Keep reading if you are wondering how to use your altar during rituals and while performing spells and magic. The following chapters will cover all you need to know about these topics and offer some interesting ways in which you can use your altar while celebrating Samhain. We will also explore Samhain's sacred herbs and plants, which can be used to decorate your altar.

By the time you have finished with the book, you will be comfortable making use of your altar for rituals and better understand how to perform Samhain rituals, both independently and with a group or coven. We shall also cover how you can personalize these rituals and prayers and how you can celebrate Samhain with non-practicing friends and family.

Chapter 5: Sacred Herbs and Plants

Plants have always played a central role in pagan practices. In ancient times, people depended on their crops to survive the winter—and did everything they could to keep these plants alive. Pagans also relied on herbs for healing—the other reason for their strong connection to the world of plants. Fortunately, contemporary pagan traditions still include the regular use of plants and herbs, which are still considered sacred within this community. Their magical properties are mostly associated with Celtic pagan holidays like Samhain. As this sabbat represents one of the best times to connect practitioners with nature and its forces, the plants linked to this holiday enjoy wide popularity. Their lore is found in all the different pagan traditions practiced nowadays.

Thanks to these ancient traditions, pagan communities worldwide can stick together. It also allowed the ranks of poets and druids to pass down their wisdom to the new generations when all other means were prohibited. Plants have played a fundamental part in this process. They were a neutral topic that carried no danger to those who opposed paganism.

Without the plant's ability to sustain life on Earth, we would not be able to thrive. However, plants and nature have to give up their life after each Samhain for this to happen. Come spring, it will be reborn anew, bringing new life. Working with the plants and herbs discussed in this chapter can also help you understand the significance of doing everything to ensure the spirits of nature will wake up refreshed in the spring.

In this chapter, you will be introduced to the main plant groups used in pagan practice. You will encounter healing herbs, plants, and herbs you can use in the kitchen, herbs to cleanse your energy, and protective plants. Keep in mind that different plants have different magical properties. Some plants in this chapter can be used for multiple purposes, while others are best used for a single purpose. Some are great for healing but may be less than useful for nutritional purposes. At the same time, others are perfect for cleansing your body, mind, and space but should never be consumed as food.

For all these reasons, it is crucial to familiarize yourself with the proper use of each. This will allow you to pick the right plants for each occasion. For example, if you want to protect yourself or your home from malicious spirits on the night of Samhain, you should use herbs associated with good spirits. These plants will invite kindred spirits into your life to have the spiritual protection and guidance you need during the sabbat of Samhain. On the other hand, if your goal is to make offerings for your spiritual allies, you'll use sacred herbs suitable for your celebratory meals. After all, offerings are typically just food you set aside from your meals to honor kindred spirits.

Rosemary

As the plant associated with remembrance, rosemary is the perfect tool for Samhain spells and rituals. According to written Roman sources, rosemary was also used at Celtic pagan ceremonies as protection from malicious spirits. In Celtic pagan communities, rosemary was also used in the homes of those who died from an infectious disease. This was part of the smudging ritual meant to purify the energy of the place and prevent the disease from spreading. Later on, priests in Christian churches adopted the use of rosemary and implemented it during religious ceremonies.

Before performing a Samhain ritual, you can use dried rosemary to cleanse your mind, body, and soul from negativity. Alternatively, you can create a charm from the fresh branches and hang it on your door. It will invite the spirits of your ancestors to your home, prompting them to join you in your Samhain celebrations and protect you from unwanted spiritual influences.

Mugwort

According to Celtic lore, mugwort is closely associated with divination. If malicious spirits torment someone in their dreams, this plant can help them block that influence. You will need to heat a large stone in an oven or fireplace, sprinkle it with dried mugwort, and pour water on top of it to create steam. Inhale this before sleeping so that the steam gets into your lungs and later evaporates, removing all the negative influences.

Another way to use mugwort is to incorporate it into the smudge sticks you'll use in your divination ritual, or you can simply place a dried batch under your pillow to receive the answer you are looking for when sleeping.

Lavender

Lavender has an incredibly relaxing aroma, so it has been used for thousands of years. Its calming effects are good for treating insomnia, anxiety, or focusing your mind when meditating. In addition, lavender oil has anti-inflammatory and antiseptic properties—perfect for treating minor wounds. For this reason, pagans often resort to using lavender in their healing practices.

While lavender can be grown indoors, its healing properties are much stronger if it has grown outside, closer to other natural elements, such as the Sun and the Moon. If you want to use lavender in preparation for the Samhain festivities or even during them, harvest the flowers at night, just before the flower buds have opened. You can also buy fresh or dried lavender. When buying it fresh, hang it upside down in a warm and dry area. After two to three weeks, shake off the buds and store them or use them immediately. Put the dried flower buds into a reusable tea bag and place it on your altar to help you focus on the spells and rituals you perform at Samhain. You can also put a packet of flowers under your pillow to help spells to take effect during the night while you are sleeping.

Peppermint

Peppermint is another popular garden herb that has been a staple in every pagan healer practice since ancient times. It is typically consumed as a tea or used throughout the year to treat a broad range of conditions, such as congestion, headache, toothache, or muscle pain. On Samhain, you can use the refreshing aroma of peppermint to gain strength for all your activities. It can also help clear your mind before summoning an ancestor so you can interpret their messages better.

You can easily grow peppermint at home, even indoors, so you have an endless supply of this beneficial plant, or you can buy fresh or dried and make your own tea, an ointment, or a healing salve. In most cases, you will need to boil it in hot water; the longer you do it, the more potent its effects will be.

Chamomile

Like peppermint, chamomile is an incredibly powerful herb with medicinal properties. This herb is only used as a soothing tea, tisane, or salve. Dried or freshly picked flowers are placed in hot boiling water, and a concoction is brewed to the required strength. The longer you brew it, the stronger it will be.

Place the dried chamomile flowers in a reusable tea bag or cheesecloth and submerge them into your bathwater on the night of Samhain. This will relieve any symptoms of stress and revitalize your skin, cleansing your body and mind from any negative energy. You can also mix chamomile with other relaxing herbs or buy it as Bio-Oil and use it for your bath. A lesser-known fact is that it can also be a source of empowerment during Samhain celebrations.

Whether you practice healing regularly or just want to give back to your community at this time of the year, chamomile is a safe way to do this. Create your own chamomile healing salve and treat skin conditions such as eczema, minor cuts, and burns.

Chrysanthemum

This flower is linked to protection, making it another appropriate plant to use at Samhain. Remember, when you invite the benevolent spirits to join you during this sabbat, they may be accompanied by some malicious ones. Chrysanthemums can help you keep the latter at bay because they bloom around this time, which means they will be full of pure, natural energy.

To ensure no harm will come to you or your loved ones, use these flowers as a centerpiece during the festivities or create a wreath you can hang on your front door. Chrysanthemums are also associated with the sun and fire, which you can use for your benefit during Samhain. Dry the flowers and use them as incense for rituals and spells requiring the power of the sun or the fire element.

Rowan Trees

Rowan is another plant used to keep unwanted spirits at bay on the night of Samhain. Branches and berries are placed outside pagan homes, and this has been performed for many years, but gifting these was also a common custom in Celtic pagan communities. You can implement either of these practices or place the branches and berries over the windows and doors—even inside your home—to protect yourself and your loved ones from evil influences.

It is also believed that planting a rowan tree near your loved one's grave allows them to move on more peacefully. This way, their spirit may guide you and the next generations in the future. If you cut the berries in half, you will notice how the inside resembles a pentagram (a traditional Celtic pagan symbol of protection). Place these around the home for added security and abundance in your life.

Apple

Samhain marks the end of the apple harvest season, and the number of apples gathered each fall was once used to represent how successful the year was. According to the Celtic pagan lore, the more apples harvested, the more likely deities and ancestral spirits would side with mortals. This also meant they were inclined to help with other matters, but only if they were properly thanked for contributing to the bountiful harvest. If you also want to express gratitude to your spiritual guide during Samhain, you can do this in several ways. You can prepare dishes with apples and offer them to your ancestors, or simply leave a basket of fresh apples on your altar as an offering.

If you can find apple branches with mature fruit and flowers, including unopened buds, use them to journey to the spiritual world. Apple flowers and the fruit itself can be used for divination. This can be particularly helpful if what you are interested in is related to your emotions. As the apples are associated with the heart, their peel may reveal something meaningful about your relationships. Likewise, the number of seeds you find in an apple may indicate a new emotional connection in your near future.

Pomegranate

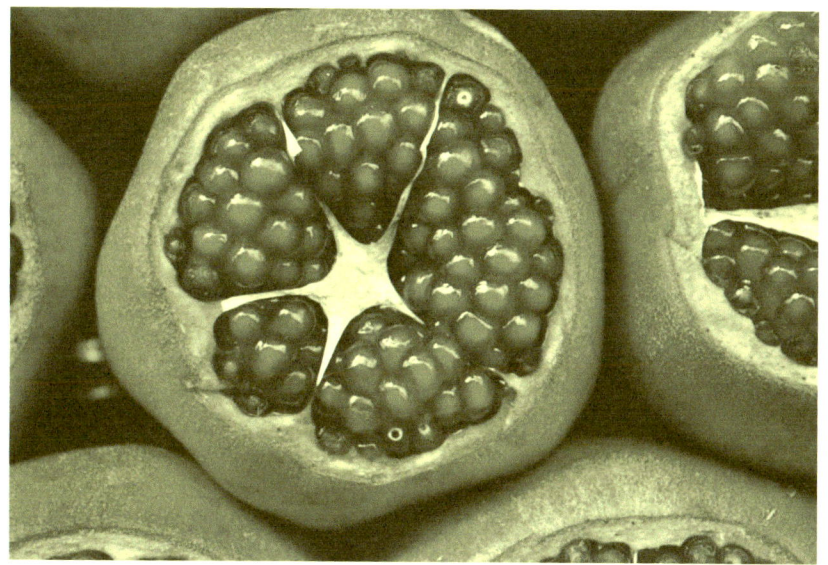

Pomegranate.
https://pixabay.com/es/photos/granada-frutas-comida-rebanado-3383814/

Thanks to their many seeds, pomegranates are often associated with fertility. Used at Samhain rituals and ceremonies, pomegranates can ensure that your next year will be even more fruitful than the current one was. Feel free to incorporate the seeds into your meals and drinks, even the ones you prepared as an offering to ask your deities and ancestral spirits to provide you with abundance.

Pomegranates are also linked to the spiritual world—due to their seeds. Their large number represents the power of nature—something you can always rely on as a pagan when trying to communicate with the spiritual world. Scoop out the seeds into a bowl and place them on your altar. Put them next to represent the spirit you are trying to communicate with, and recite the appropriate spell over them.

Lemon

Lemon has been used as a natural remedy for many conditions and should never be limited to only being used in the kitchen. Its high vitamin content boosts the immune system, making this fruit essential to fight off infections. Lemon is also packed with antioxidants, whether used in raw form or as an oil. However, lemons can be used for much more than soothing a sore throat during the winter or as a refreshing drink in the scorching summer heat.

Lemon trees are not the easiest to grow, so you will most likely get the fruit from a shop or market. If you buy the fruit, get organic lemons to enjoy all their benefits. You can use lemons or lemon juice to prepare light desserts or dressings for the wild meat dishes traditionally prepared for the Samhain festivities. Lemon oil can be used for cleansing baths, meditation, or anointing your candles.

Squashes and Pumpkins

Squashes and pumpkins are also well-known indicators of abundance during the harvest season. Harvested late in the season, they have become a staple decoration for pagans and non-pagans all around the globe. However, these fall fruits can have more purpose than simply being a funky decoration during the Samhain festivities. They can be stored in many forms, providing plenty of nourishment for many more months.

At Samhain, you can incorporate them into your meals or use them for divination purposes. Carving a symbol of protection into the skin of a squash or pumpkin and leaving the carved fruit outside your door or window is another ancient pagan custom you can implement to keep unwanted spirits at bay.

Aloe Vera

Due to its remarkable healing properties, aloe vera has been used for centuries. People from all around the world are raving about the sticky gel you can find inside this plant. It relieves pain, speeds up healing of the skin, and has a moisturizing effect. This beneficial plant can also be incorporated into pagan practices, including the celebration of Samhain.

One of the best things about aloe vera is that it grows indoors. It is one of those plants that thrive on neglect, so you will not have to worry about watering it. Place the plant in moderate sunlight for a stylish decoration, a relaxing sight, and an immediate supply of aloe vera gel whenever you need it. To harvest it, cut off one of the mature leaves and let the yellow liquid drain from it—rinse it with water to speed up the process. Use a clean, sharp knife to remove the edges of the leaf and the top and bottom pieces of its skin. You'll find a translucent gel you can immediately apply to the skin underneath it. If you do not want to use it right away, scoop out the gel, freeze it, cut it into small cubes, and store it in the freezer for up to a month.

Apply the gel onto your skin as a moisturizer after taking a traditional Samhain bath, or use the plant as a tool to relax your mind when preparing for a spell or ritual. The gel can also treat minor burns during the Samhain bonfire ritual.

Tips for Implementing Sacred Herbs and Plants into Your Practice

Depending on the paganism you practice, you may find some ancient customs—such as gifting each other with plant products, including fruit, leaves, and nectar—very much alive within your community. If you do not live in a pagan community or are just delving into this topic, you may find incorporating plants and herbs into your practice challenging. After all, we are no longer dependent on the harvest season because we can find all the produce we need throughout the year in supermarkets, so we often take nature for granted. In this case, you should try to connect with nature through meditation and deep breathing techniques performed amid a patch of nature. Regardless of where you live, you can always find a little green corner to admire nature's work more closely. It will help you appreciate everything the sacred herbs and plants can give you around Samhain.

Moreover, as you observe nature around you, you will be reminded that you are just as much a part of nature as all the greenery you see and the animals feeding on it are. If it is not a protected area, you may even take a few herbal souvenirs when you go home to familiarize yourself with their texture, scent, and colors, or you can simply visit a market and buy some herbs you can experiment with in your budding practice. While you can do this at any time of the year, you must remember that Samhain marks the height of the harvest season. This means that the fresh plants are the most potent at this time of the year—making this sabbat perfect for learning all about them.

One of the best ways to start including sacred herbs and plants in your practice is to prepare a celebratory meal. As you can see from the individual description of the plants, Samhain meals typically use many fruits, vegetables, and foraged goods. However, herbs used as spices also play a significant part in these meals. It's a good idea to establish a home garden. No matter how small the space you have for it is, the plants you can grow in your garden will make you appreciate the true meaning of this harvest festival. You can also use herbs to anoint candles before casting your spells and initiating your rituals. Alternatively, you can opt for pampering yourself in a bath using dried, relaxing, or invigorating herbs and oils made from them.

It's important to note that if you are allergic to any of the plants mentioned in this chapter, you should not use them in your practices. If you are not sure whether you have a sensitivity or not, it's always a good idea to do a patch test before using them. Do this for any new plant or herb you will try, whether fresh, dry, or in oil form. People with certain conditions are advised not to use specific herbs or essential oils, which may aggravate their condition. Some herbs can adversely affect healthy pregnant women and their unborn children, who should not use them. If pregnant or breastfeeding, consult a health care professional regarding what plants are safe for consumption.

Chapter 6: Celebrating with Food

We all love festivals and celebrations. We get to have a great time, and they also remind us where we come from and who we are. Festivals are a great way to bring people together and remind us that, despite our differences or backgrounds, we are united by the things we celebrate despite our differences. Festivals also allow us to share a part of who we are with friends and family members who have different beliefs or who practice other traditions. They are great opportunities to teach children about the essence of tradition and make them feel involved. Most importantly, celebrations play a great role in helping us keep our cultures and traditions alive.

Most celebrations in the world come with a menu of their own. Food is an integral part of all cultures across the globe. Food is more than just the mouth-watering, delectable part of the experience. It is of utmost significance when it comes to ensuring that a tradition lives on for generations to come. Nothing strengthens the bonds within a community more than coming together to share a meal that holds significance to each person.

Hosting a dinner or cooking a meal to enjoy on the day of the celebration is a great way to express your love and gratitude to those who are invited. It also makes you feel like you have accomplished something great during the festival. No matter whom you are inviting, the food you cook always sends a message, whether it is "I care for you," "I want to share a part of who I am with you," or "I'm grateful that I get to celebrate with you."

Food is an integral part of the experience if you're celebrating alone. You do not need to host a huge dinner, or even eat with your family, to cook holiday or festival-related meals. It's an opportunity to press pause on the strenuous nature of daily life and take a moment to "savor" the moments that truly matter and get into the true spirit of the celebration with a special menu. Any festival is incomplete without its unique set of food items. In this chapter, you will come across a wide range of recipes you can cook on Samhain to relish on your own or share with your friends, family, or neighbors. These are guaranteed to help you feel the true essence of the celebration and get the full, authentic Samhain experience, especially once you learn why each recipe is relevant to the festival. Here, you will also come across the different Samhain dining methods, highlighting the different ways you can enjoy a meal traditionally on the day of the celebration.

Samhain Food Recipes

As you know, Samhain is typically a community-centered festival. This is because it usually involves group ceremonies and bonfires, making feasts a natural piece of the celebratory pie. However, there are numerous ways to celebrate Samhain by yourself, and cooking up a festival-relevant meal is definitely one of them.

Samhain is celebrated with a wide range of food items. Besides highlighting the end of the season of light or harvest, the festival honors the passage of loved ones. This is why meals are often cooked, and plates are served to honor those no longer celebrating with us. Since the festival also marks the end of the harvest season, it also makes sense that a feast should be prepared.

Samhain is an ancient practice that has been celebrated for centuries; thus, many traditional recipes have been swept away with time. However, there is still a wide range of recipes and ingredients that you can use to keep the festival's spirit alive. Recipes mainly focus on fall produce and seasonal foods, which will become scarcer throughout the year. Most dishes contain flavorful ingredients like pumpkins, cruciferous vegetables, potatoes, and apples.

Ancient Celts based their harvesting habits and traditions on the farming calendar. They brought all their cattle in during the colder months of the year. It is also said that they slaughtered the livestock during the harsh winter instead of feeding them. This is why meat was also a ubiquitous dish among herding communities at that time of year. Potatoes and oats were dug up and stacked for the fest.

For some people, the festival's menu had to do with story-telling traditions and unique beliefs. For instance, many people worried that the púca (a fairy and shapeshifter) would spit on their produce if it were not collected before Samhain. To this day, some Irish people are still in the habit of leaving out a meal for the fairies to enjoy on Samhain. They often leave a plate of champ and a spoon at the foot of a hawthorn tree. Another tradition is to bake thick oatcakes with holes in the middle so that string can be threaded through them. Children who would go "trick-or-treating" to collect nuts and apples from their neighbors would also leave with an oatcake necklace.

Samhain is a time that is very closely tied to deep reflection. It's an opportunity to look back on all you have achieved throughout the past year and develop goals and plans for the coming period. This is a time when terms like "safe," "wellness," "comfort," and "coziness" are highly relevant. The typical Samhain menu reflects these themes of protection and comfort, considering the warming nature of the flavors and ingredients used. Many recipes are roasted, simmered, casseroled, or roasted. Others are seasoned with cinnamon, rosemary, sage, nutmeg, or even garnished with nuts. The food at this time of year is exciting, filling, delicious, and soul-stirring. The following are some traditional Samhain recipes you can prepare for your celebrations.

Soul Cakes

Soul cakes are commonly served on Samhain. Their association with the festival is uncertain; however, they were originally baked for charity. On the night of the sabbat, the poorer citizens of a town would visit the homes of the wealthy, asking for money or food. They offered to pray for the homeowner's loved ones who had passed away in return for an act of kindness. Soul cakes were usually given to the beggars as blessings. There are numerous soul cake recipes, so one version of a soul cake may differ greatly from another. Here is one quick yet delicious way to make this popular delicacy:

Ingredients:

- 1 softened stick of butter
- 1 ½ cups of flour
- 4 tbsp. of sugar

Instructions:

1. In a bowl, place the softened butter and the sugar and stir well until you are left with a creamy mixture.
2. Add the flour to the bowl using a flour sifter. Mix once more and ensure that the dough is lump-free.
3. Divide the dough in half and shape each half into a circle. Use a rolling pin to spread it out. Each circle should be half an inch thick.
4. Place the dough on an ungreased baking sheet and use a fork to draw lines in the dough. Each half should have eight wedges.
5. Set the oven to 350 degrees Fahrenheit and bake the cakes for twenty-five minutes or until they are light brown.

Colcannon

Colcannon is another favorite dish among those who celebrate Samhain. This dish has been ingrained as part of the tradition probably because its ingredients are in season (potatoes and greens like kale and cabbage). This side dish will make a great addition to your dinner table.

Ingredients:

- 5 medium-sized Yokun Gold potatoes
- 2 diced leeks (use only the white and light green parts)
- 6 tbsp. unsalted butter
- 2 thinly-sliced garlic cloves
- Kosher salt (to taste)
- 2 cups of packed, shredded savoy cabbage
- 1¼ cups of milk
- ½ a cup of heavy cream
- Freshly ground black pepper
- 1 thinly-sliced scallion

Instructions:

1. Place the potatoes in a small pot, cover them with water, and season with a dash of salt. Turn up the heat to medium-high and bring to a boil. Turn down the heat and let the potatoes simmer. Once done, drain the potatoes, let them cool slightly, and then peel. Use a knife to check if it slices right through (you should be able to do that within thirty to forty minutes).

2. As the potatoes cook, put a large saucepan over medium-high heat and melt four tablespoons of butter. Drop in the leeks and let them cook for eight to ten minutes, stirring in between.

3. Once they soften up, add the garlic and stir until fragrant. The edges of the leeks should start browning within three minutes. Afterward, add a cup of cabbage and stir until it has wilted. Add the cream and milk and bring the ingredients to

a simmer.

4. Add the potatoes and the other cup of cabbage. Use a masher to mash the potatoes coarsely. Season with salt and pepper.
5. Move the colcannon to a serving bowl and top it off with the rest of the butter and the scallions.

Barmbrack

This traditional dish happens to be a traditional Irish bread recipe. This type of bread is associated with Samhain because it includes trinkets that serve as a form of fortune-telling. For instance, if someone gets a ring, it means they will get married within the coming year. A coin symbolizes wealth, the cloth is associated with hardship, and dry peas resemble a dry wedding spell (no weddings). You can always use trinkets of your own choice!

Ingredients:

- 2 beaten eggs
- 1 large lemon zest
- 1 large orange zest
- 2 cups of hot, strong black breakfast tea
- 3 cups of all-purpose flour
- 1 cup of dark brown sugar
- 2 tsp of baking powder
- 1 tsp of mixed spice (you can also use pumpkin pie spice)
- 1 3/4 cups of raisins
- 1 3/4 cups of sultanas
- Dried fruit

Instructions:

1. Preheat the oven to 325 degrees Fahrenheit.
2. Line and butter a deep nine-inch cake pan and set it aside.
3. Add the sultanas, orange zest, lemon zest, raisins, and sugar to a medium-sized bowl. Pour the tea and mix well. Place cling film over the bowl and leave it at room temperature to set overnight.
4. Place the spices, baking powder, and flour in a large bowl and mix well.
5. Add your dried fruits and eggs. Whisk together until there are no dry streaks.

6. Wrap your trinkets in parchment paper and add them to the mixture.
7. Pour the batter into a lined and buttered pan.
8. Leave the bread to bake for 80 to 90 minutes or until golden. It should spring back up when lightly pressed.
9. Let it cool for twenty minutes and take it out of the pan.
10. Slice it to your desired thickness and serve with butter.

Samhain Dining Methods

There are numerous ways to celebrate Samhain through food. Since this is a communal festival, we recommend that you host a large feast and invite your community over. If you do not know anyone who celebrates Samhain, you can use this as an opportunity to share your beliefs and traditions with your loved ones. You can introduce the concept of Samhain to your close friends or family members and ask them to celebrate this festival with you. You can choose a few of the recipes mentioned above and have them experience the spirit of Samhain with you.

If your neighborhood celebrates the festival, you can all participate in a bonfire ritual and eat afterward. You can also have a large outdoor gathering at night where each person cooks up a traditional dish. However, the most popular way to dine on Samhain is to have a silent (dumb) supper.

Having your dinner in silence is a great way to honor the dead, particularly family members or friends who passed away the previous year. Silent suppers are also commonly held for any ancestral spirits that anyone attending wishes to pay their respects to. The origins of dumb suppers are not very clear. However, according to some sources, this tradition is derived from the Ozarks. Others claim that it originated in the Appalachian Mountains. Regardless of how this tradition came about, it was a very popular practice among neopagans at the time of Samhain.

Hosting a Dumb Supper

The idea of a dumb supper may seem incredibly odd to those still learning about the Sabbats. However, the more you reflect on the practice, the better you will understand the idea behind it. Silent suppers are a great way to acknowledge and reflect on your thoughts, considering this is a time of deep reflection. Think about your deceased loved ones, pay them your respects, and express your gratitude toward those in your life today. The Wheel of the Year and its sabbats represent the cyclical nature of life. Death, an inevitable part of life, is one of the hardest things to grasp and accept. We feel lost, mournful, and depressed after the people we love exit our lives. Samhain presents an opportunity to alleviate some of these emotions and lessen the sense of grief by feeling the presence of those who passed and celebrating with people who care about us.

Dumb suppers may seem inherently depressing. However, there are numerous ways in which you can make them more enjoyable and much more exciting. For instance, you are free to design your invitations in whatever way you like. You can also do the same with the table favors. Find a way to maintain the solemn nature of the event, yet convey the spirit of the festivities. Play around with tiny wooden coffins and even Halloween decorations. You can also use obituary-themed menus and invitations!

Invitations and the Guests of Honor

You need to put in some thought to decide whom you want to invite to your dumb supper. You should also consider inviting children. However, in that case, you will have to make some changes to the overall course of the celebration. You will find more on that in the following chapter. While this can be a great way to introduce your children and other kids in the family to the concept of death, it can be a very difficult topic for them to grasp. You should also discuss whether other parents are open to bringing their children over, especially since children will not remain silent for the entire thirty- to forty-minute duration of the dinner.

You should also determine whom you want your guest of honor to be. This is usually a person who has passed away in the last year. You should set a place for them at the head of the table, marking it with a photograph or any other unique way to represent them. For instance, you can honor them by placing the things they enjoyed in life, such as their favorite book, an instrument they played, or a symbol of their favorite hobby, on the chair. If you do not wish to honor one specific person, the head of the table can be symbolically set to represent numerous guests of honor. Since finding things that represent all the people you wish to pay your respects to will not be possible, you can represent them through a universal symbol, like a candle. You can represent each guest using a candle in their favorite color.

The Atmosphere

The heart of any festival or celebration lies in the general atmosphere. This is why you can try to make the environment mysterious. To set the mood, you can use black tablecloths, candles, and tableware. You can also light up the space using candles and lanterns and even use ingredients like activated charcoal to create a black cocktail. You will find many variations of the recipe online. Using fire for lighting is a great idea since it not only helps you create an eerie ambiance, but many people believe that artificial light sources hinder spirit communication. You should keep all technological devices turned off throughout the dinner.

The Food

Any recipes mentioned above would be appropriate to serve during a dumb dinner. If one of the guests of honor used to cook traditional Samhain recipes, you can include them in the menu. If they don't celebrate Samhain, you can tweak their recipes and add certain spices or legumes to give them a more seasonal feel. If you wish, you can also figure out a way to change the color of some of the dishes to black without affecting their taste—if you decide to go with an all-black theme. If you are hosting a large dinner, it can be very hard to cook everything yourself. In that case, you can turn it into a potluck. You can create a list to avoid repetition.

Silence Level

Silence is crucial because it helps heighten the senses and guide us toward the spiritual world. Make sure to mention explicitly that the dinner will be held in complete silence upon invitation. That way, everyone will know in advance.

When setting up the table, ensure you prepare everything, so verbal communication is minimized. You can serve the plates and ensure that they are well-portioned to avoid having bowls passed around, which can be distracting and noisy. This will require you to take note of everyone's allergies, dietary needs, and preferences. If you want, you can set up an open buffet on a separate table so people can choose what they wish to eat. Once everyone has their plates ready, you can all sit down and start the dumb supper. Make sure you explain that no one can get up for refills once you start.

Social events where everyone is quiet are typically very awkward. However, it is very different when you attend a ritual where no words are needed. You can just sit down, enjoy everyone's presence, savor the food, and reflect without worrying about the next thing to say. It is certainly an experience of a lifetime.

Communicating with Departed Loved Ones

Use this opportunity to communicate with your departed loved ones. It does not matter if you don't believe in an afterlife. You can view this as a chance to let go of the things you never had the chance to tell them. Some people like to write messages on pieces of paper to burn them in a cauldron. However, it's not recommended to do so indoors. You can burn them on an outdoor bonfire after dinner if you would like.

Having a bonfire is a great excuse to get the party going. Everyone can go back to socializing afterward. You can have drinks, read tarot cards, share memories, and make the experience all the more enjoyable. Make sure you fold some Samhain-relevant herbs like sage or cinnamon into the paper and use the herb and essential oil to anoint it before throwing it into the fire.

Food is an integral part of all celebrations and festivals worldwide. It is a great way to revive ancient traditions and keep them going for centuries. It also serves to share your beliefs or culture with your friends and family. You can say a lot just by serving others a meal. Now that you have read this chapter, you are ready to host a memorable Samhain feast.

Chapter 7: Family and Group Activities

Host dinner with your family for Samhain to honor the dead.
https://www.pexels.com/photo/selective-focus-photography-of-man-preparing-food-beside-smiling-women-and-kids-3171151/

Festivals are an important part of Wiccan and Druid community life. People born into Wicca and Druidry worldwide grow up celebrating festivals, regarding them as an integral aspect of life. There are eight pagan festivals, each symbolizing seasonal changes that Wiccans celebrate worldwide.

Despite their religious and cultural significance, festivals are celebrated for various reasons. Neopagans view them as an opportunity to unite the community and reinforce the sense of belonging and togetherness. This time unites all pagans as they celebrate a certain purpose or time of the year.

Besides the excitement and fun, festivals make great learning opportunities for kids. Even though they may not always understand, children enjoy festivals the most. They are introduced to games, decorations, preparations, gifts, and sweets. Celebrating with other friends and family makes your kids excited to see everyone come together.

Samhain allows the family to bond over meaningful experiences. They can all participate in something they truly believe in. This is a great chance to get your kids involved in important events. You can encourage them to help you with the decorations and food preparations. This strengthens familial bonds and reminds us of the things that matter.

Depending on how you choose to celebrate, festivals are associated with exchanging gifts and sharing. This creates a joyous atmosphere and encourages children to donate their old toys or help the less fortunate. You can celebrate Samhain in endless ways! Besides the main traditions tied to this festival, you can use this time to teach your kids about important values like generosity, gratefulness, kindness, and humbleness. You can also remind your kids of their roots and family history by honoring your ancestors on that day. At the end of the day, Samhain is the perfect time to let go of old, unhelpful habits to make way for new and healthier ones.

There is no better way to teach your children about your beliefs than celebrating with them during festivals. During this time, they are likely to learn certain concepts and ideas that they otherwise would not be able to wrap their heads around. Traditional activities and celebrations prompt kids to explore because of their natural curiosity. They will probably inquire about certain rituals or ask why things are done a certain way. This is why stories are shared and oral traditions come to life during the sabbats. You can get your kids excited by helping them understand the significance of these festivals through the generations.

Even if you do not have children, celebrating Samhain can be a great way to reconnect with your community and celebrate your similarities. It's not every day that we find people who share our beliefs and traditions. This is why hosting or going to Samhain gatherings and participating in similar social activities can be quite fulfilling. This chapter will find plenty of family-friendly and social activities to try during Samhain. You will also learn how to throw a Samhain or "New Year" party!

Celebrating with Family

The following are a few families and kid-friendly ways to celebrate Samhain and embrace its spirit:

Set Intentions

As mentioned, Samhain is all about letting go of the old and paving the way for new and more fruitful opportunities. Gather your family around and ask them to write down any intrusive thoughts, feelings, and unhealthy habits they are struggling with. Encourage your children to write down anything that comes to mind, no matter how small it is. Perhaps they wish to stop telling lies or being messy. Once all of you complete your list, throw it into the Samhain fire. Do not forget to state your intentions—letting go of bad habits, emotions, and feelings to create space for better ones. Now that you have done that start writing another list comprising your dreams and ideas for the following year. If you want, you can share the things you wrote down with the rest of the family. If anyone wants to keep them to themselves, keep the lists safe until spring, giving them extra attention during winter.

Get Crafty

You can do several crafts with your family to celebrate Samhain. For instance, you can use seasonal symbols like corns and pumpkins to decorate the festival's altar. You can keep the celebrations going for the entire season, considering that your children will be coming home earlier than they usually do—shorter days and longer nights, remember? Doing simple crafts with just a few supplies is the perfect way to keep them busy and engaged while celebrating. Harvest crafts are very popular during this Sabbat. Go out with your family and gather some leaves. You can get as creative as you want! Paint them in bright colors and use them to make leaf prints or glue them together to create a picture. You can carve pumpkins or even make necklaces out of acorns.

Get Outside

The lights may be going out early, but this does not mean you should not embrace the change of seasons. Grab your jacket and head out for a moonlight walk with your family or have a small bonfire. Build a fire and toast marshmallows while sharing stories about the festival and your ancestors. Ensure you check whether there are any hibernating animals while raking through the things you are going to burn and be careful while handling the fire.

Go for a hike and discuss with your kids why some animals hibernate in winter or why the leaves fall and change color. You can also go for a run to welcome the new season with high activity levels. We usually get lazier during winter, so that is one way to set things off on the right track. Encourage your family to maintain healthy habits throughout the following year. When you're out, make sure you observe and give your thanks to the world around you. Express your gratitude toward the changing seasons and the coming of fall. You can do that in whichever way you desire. You can pray silently, give back to the community, help the less fortunate, meditate in nature, or even yodel in your backyard!

Honor Your Ancestors

Honoring your ancestors and recalling the memories are among the most important aspects of Samhain. The stories you tell and how you plan to approach this idea depend on your kids' ages. If you believe they are too young to understand complex matters like life and death, you can always postpone this tradition to the following year. However, many people view this festival as an opportunity to introduce their children to their origins and ancestors.

If you have not done so already, you can study genealogy and trace back your roots with your children. Have them call their grandparents and ask them if they—or their parents or any other distant relatives—come from other countries. Have them ask them about their childhood and how different things were back in the day. Create a family tree on an ancestor altar cloth using the information you gather.

Light a candle and gather your family around to express your love, prayers, and gratitude to your loved ones. You can also set up an ancestor altar and include photos and heirlooms of those who have passed. Use natural objects, drawings, cutouts, etc., to decorate the altar.

Hold a Ritual

Rituals are usually very challenging to attend to when you have unoccupied kids around, so the best thing to do is get them involved in helping you set everything up. You can also tweak existing rituals or develop new ones to ensure that the process is fun but maintains its spiritual aspect. Before starting, ask your children how they would like to get involved. Some kids would like to participate silently, while others prefer to participate in chants and bang on a drum.

Set up a basic altar—you can use your Halloween decorations. Use candles unless you cannot trust your kids around them. Alternatively, you can use LED tea lights. If you are not setting up an ancestral altar, you can add the pictures and heirlooms of your deceased family members. If you like, you can serve food as an offering. Ask your kids to help you bake the bread beforehand. Prepare a cup of something to drink that you can share with all your family and gather around to think about those who have passed away, current family members, and loved ones.

Start the ritual by setting your intention—celebrating the lives of loved ones who have crossed over—and say the names of the people you wish to honor. Start by naming those who have died recently, working your way backward. You do not need to name every deceased person in your family tree; however, you can go into detail by mentioning how certain family members impacted your life, sharing funny or remarkable incidents, or explaining what they were like. Once done, pass the plate around, so each family member has a piece of food to use as an offering. Each person should approach the altar on their own—eldest to youngest, leaving the offering on a plate. Send out a prayer that carries your intention. You can help younger kids with the offerings and the prayer. Hold the cup and set your intention. Then take a sip and pass it to the next person. Put the cup on the altar, join hands, close your eyes, thank your ancestors, and take a moment to reflect. End the rite in whatever way you prefer.

Have Fun!

Samhain and Halloween are deeply connected for most of us, which is totally fine! This time of the year, in particular, is a crossover between the mundane and the spiritual, and this is probably why your children will likely want to bridge this gap in one way or another. Just as you wish to celebrate Samhain, they are probably more interested in the Halloween festivities. Luckily for you, you can trick-or-treat and dress up in any costumes you like while still making plenty of time for the spiritual aspect of Samhain.

You can suggest mixing it up at Halloween in your neighborhood. Instead of having children knock on individual doors down the street, you can throw one large party. Offer food and candy to anyone who walks by! One person can grill on their porch, their neighbor can offer the beverages, another can layout the desserts, and so on. Have one large bonfire and share stories or read spooky Samhain-related poems! Interacting with the community, having a barbeque, and sharing candy with adults can be twice as much fun.

Extend the Celebrations

Celebrations are always more tasteful when your loved ones are around. Invite your neighbors, friends, and family for a feast of various harvest foods. You can even ask your guests to bring a dish so you can share. Spending time with your community and interacting with others is always a great way to celebrate Samhain. If you wish, you can even celebrate in the traditional Celtic way. Celebrate for three days, just like they did back then. Hold rituals and dances, and have feasts during that time. These are all ways to connect with the energy of Samhain.

Group Activities

The following are some ways in which you can celebrate Samhain with a group of people:

Have a Silent Supper

Dumb (or silent) suppers were a popular tradition, especially during the Middle Ages. Eating a meal in complete silence is considered a way in which you can honor your ancestors. Beside your dining table, you can set up another table with pictures, memorials, and heirlooms of loved ones who have crossed over. You can decorate the table with flowers, candles, and tablecloths. Make sure you pick out symbolic colors or choose ones that tie back to a certain memory. Add extra plates for the souls that you wish to honor. Light the candles and have your dinner in complete silence to welcome the spirits. This is because they are very sensitive to the energies in the room. Take this time to think back to your memories, reflect on your emotion, and express your thankfulness and gratitude (silently).

Light Things Up

During Samhain, the Celts held a large communal fire in the village. They gathered around it and went home with a burning branch so they could see each light in their hearth. Villages typically lit several communal fires around them because they believed it would help guide the spirits to their homes. You can have your own bonfire if you want, but this may be a bit of a stretch. You need to have enough space and, of course, the knowledge on how to build, tend, and handle a fire. This is something you can do with a large group of people to reignite the spirit of Samhain. Alternatively, you can pay special attention to your home lighting. Use candles, purchase new lamps, and decorate your home with colored lights, which is something that can also be turned into a group activity!

Create Centerpieces

Gather your friends around and create Samhain-themed centerpieces to place on tables, mantels, altars, or windowsills as decorations. Use black, red, white, and orange candles, tourmaline, amber, obsidian, or similar crystals, fallen leaves, pine cones, and corn dolls. Ask your friends to think of all their achievements. Tell them to think about the centerpieces you are about to make to remind them to honor all they have achieved. You can even use Halloween decorations.

Hold a Moon Circle

Gather your fellow neopagans and stand under Samhain's bright moonlight. Grab a huge spiral and pour salt and nuts inside. Place a candle in the center of the spiral. Stand at the spiral's edge in a circle, all joining hands. Walk toward the center of the spiral. At this point, everyone should push something bad from the past year out of their mind. If this would make it easier, you can write down the things you wish to leave behind. Scatter the pieces of paper as you move around. Light the candle and have each person grab a nut before moving out of the center of the spiral. The nut is representative of seeds, allowing for new beginnings and energies and making way for growth. Think about your intentions for the coming year as you do so.

How to Host a Samhain Party

If you wish to host a Samhain party to celebrate the New Year, this book is here to help! Before you start planning, you need to decide whether you will invite kids to the party. If most of your community has children, you will probably find that you have to. Thu, you will need to choose kid-friendly activities and decor. At the very least, you will have to consult with the parents about whether they would like their children to participate in the ritual. In that case, you may want to tweak the process to make it more kid-friendly. You should also select at least one of the family-friendly activities mentioned in this chapter to keep them occupied.

Then, you should determine your main event for the party. Dumb suppers are a great way to honor the deceased and your ancestors. However, they may not work if you have children around. You can hold a séance instead. Choosing one main event will allow you to stick to a specific theme. However, you can always hold both.

Plan out additional smaller activities for your party. This will make your party memorable and ideal for parents who have kids around. Pumpkin carving or acorn necklace contests can be great bonding experiences. Ensure everyone feels included.

Acknowledge your ancestors by including a few photographs and heirlooms on the altar. You should do that, especially if someone has recently lost a loved one. If you are holding a ritual, your guests probably will not be anticipating a wide range of food options. You can offer fall-related appetizers and simple dishes. If you are hosting a dumb supper, you'll have to go all out. Ask your guests to bring a dish along.

If you're not inviting children, consider lighting up the place using just fire. You can use a blend of bonfires, candles, and tiki torches to create the ambiance. Use natural decorations instead of sticking to the basic Halloween ornaments. Ornament the scene with pumpkins, acorns, pine cones, etc.

Finally, make Samhain ritual favors. There are endless options that you can choose from.

Samhain is among the most significant festivals in neopagan society. If you're part of the Wiccan or Druid community, you may have someone to celebrate Samhain and the other sabbats or festivals. The more the people around, the greater the joy that everyone experiences. Celebrating Samhain with friends, family, or other community members teaches the kids the need for society and the wonders of working with one another for a certain cause. Allowing them to partake in the preparations for Samhain can help them realize that they are important community members and encourages them to find their place in it. They are also taught the basics of shared responsibilities, delegation, and teamwork. They understand that when everyone puts in the work, great things happen. Even if you do not have kids, you can still experience the great joys of the festival. At the very least, you can host your own New Year party and view this as an opportunity to let go of negative habits, thoughts, and emotions to plant the seeds for new and positive ones.

Chapter 8: Samhain Rituals and Ceremonies

Some of the previous chapters discussed how to celebrate Samhain on a physical level. We have covered building a Samhain altar and how you can celebrate with your family and friends, including non-practicing loved ones. We've even covered some foods you can include in a Samhain meal or feast.

However, celebrating Samhain often involves more than just the physical; it also involves your spiritual side. This chapter will cover everything you need to know about rituals and ceremonies you can include in your celebration and why they can play an important part in your observance of the day.

Samhain is a day of honoring the ancestors, the forgotten dead, and the people who have gone before you. It is also a time to celebrate the deities, especially those associated with the harvest and the god and goddess. In the Wheel of the Year, Samhain marks when the Horned God dies before being resurrected on Yule/the Winter Solstice; therefore, it is also when practitioners celebrate and honor the cycle of life and death.

This chapter will also cover rituals and ceremonies for solitary practitioners and those who practice in groups or covens. For those hoping to introduce their children to the spiritual side of Samhain, it will also cover some kid-friendly rituals you can try.

Note that Samhain rituals often involve acknowledging some elements of the season aloud. You can create your own script for these acknowledgments, find pre-made ones that fit your beliefs, or simply speak from your heart—ultimately, your intent matters more than getting the words perfectly right.

Set Up and Decorate Your Altar

We have already covered constructing a Samhain altar in an earlier chapter, and you can use that chapter as a guide on how to go about setting up your altar. Many people find the process of building their altar to be a spiritually significant one in itself, and it is also something you can do with children or loved ones.

If you are building your altar with a child, use this as an opportunity to explore why you're choosing certain elements to add to the sacred space. You can construct either a Samhain altar, an ancestor altar, or both.

When building your ancestor altar, you can take the opportunity to share stories about your loved ones and ancestors with those around you. You can also take the chance of asking the people you are sharing this ritual with—such as your child or family members—if they have any additions they would like to add to the altar, such as a beloved pet or someone else who has made a difference in their lives.

Solitary practitioners can take the opportunity to speak the story of each person added to the altar out loud—these stories can help charge the altar with energy.

Celebrate the Circle of Life and Death

Samhain, and all the other major sabbats, help mark key moments in the cycle of life, death, and rebirth. Samhain is the day of the Horned God's symbolic death before he is reborn on December 21 (Yule). This makes this day the perfect time to think upon—and celebrate—this key cycle that helps nurture the world.

Ideally, a ritual to celebrate the cycle of life and death should be performed outside, though you can do so inside if there is no other option.

You Will Need:
- A few sprigs of rosemary
- A white and black candle
- Black, red, and white ribbons (there should be a set of three equal length ribbons for each person participating in the ritual)
- An altar

You can perform this ritual as a solitary practitioner or with a group of other practitioners.

Instructions:
1. Decorate your altar with symbols of life and death
2. Start the ritual by casting a circle if it is part of your regular practice.
3. Start by welcoming Samhain and the approaching winter. Acknowledge the day as one of death and dying, during which you honor the ancestors, the Dark Mother, and the Ancient Ones.
4. Place the rosemary on your altar. If performing this ritual as part of a coven or group, pass the rosemary around first and ensure everyone handles it. Rosemary is a symbol of remembrance, and when placing the sprigs on the altar, vocally acknowledge the night as one on which you remember the people who have gone before you.
5. Turn to the north and welcome the spirits of the earth, who symbolize death.
6. Turn to the east and welcome the spirits of the air, who will be by a living being's side as they depart the world of the living.
7. Turn to the south and welcome the spirits of the air, who will transform the dead into death.
8. Turn to the west and welcome the water spirits, who will carry all living beings through the river of life.
9. Light the black candle and acknowledge the turning of the Wheel of the Year into darkness.

10. Light the white candle and acknowledge that light awaits at the end of darkness.
11. Each person should take their set of ribbons. White stands for life, black for death, and red for rebirth; you should acknowledge this symbolism and the memory of those you have lost. After doing so, start braiding the ribbons together. Focus on the memories of lost loved ones while doing so.
12. While you braid, vocally acknowledge the cycle of life, death, and rebirth.
13. The knotted ribbons should be placed on each person's personal altar or another place of significance for each individual.

Ancestor Meditation Ritual

Samhain is a time to honor the dead and commune with those who have gone before. The thin veil between the worlds makes it the best time of year to communicate with the dead.

One technique people often find effective when communing with the dead is meditation. Remember that everyone's experience during meditation differs, and you may find it easier to communicate with loved ones who have passed through the veil through another method.

While some people can commune with specific loved ones, others find meditation provides a way to communicate with archetypes representing the dead. For example, if someone you loved was a war veteran, you may encounter another veteran from the same war rather than the specific person you are thinking of. However, communing and meeting these individuals is still a gift and one that you should honor. They often choose to appear to people to provide them with specific messages, so pay attention to what they tell you and how they act.

Do not perform this meditation ritual with expectations—this is a time to think of everyone who has gone before you, both the good and bad. Some of your ancestors would have been great people, but others may not have been that great—and that is okay. Each of them played some part in shaping the person you are today, and this is a chance to think of them all.

If you find meditation works for you, the first step in an ancestor meditation ritual is to set the mood. Take some time going through old photo albums and keepsakes, allowing you to absorb the energies of those you have lost.

This ritual can be performed anywhere, though night is preferable. Firstly, build your ancestor altar—if performing the ritual outdoors, erect a temporary one on a flat rock or tree stump. Then decorate it. Also feel free to light a candle or some incense.

Then, sit—or stand, though sitting is more comfortable—and close your eyes, breathing deeply. Take a moment to reflect, keeping in mind that you embody the ancestors and loved ones who have come before you. Think about the strengths and weaknesses of your family members and how they have all come together in you.

Recite your genealogy as far back as possible, naming each person you're thinking of and giving a succinct description of their life and importance to you. You should also acknowledge the ancestors you do not know but who are still part of you.

As mentioned, you may encounter an ancestor or archetype during this meditation. If you do, ensure to thank them for visiting. While their words and actions may not make sense immediately, they are important, and you may find you understand better later, so make a note of what they say and do.

Plan a Cemetery Celebration

As mentioned, Samhain is a time of honoring the dead, and one way to do so is by visiting their grave at the cemetery. If you can, visit your loved ones and tend to their graves, keeping memories of the time you spent with them in mind. You can also place an offering on their graves, such as a fresh bouquet of flowers, dried herbs—especially those associated with Samhain, such as rosemary and sage—or freshwater. You can also leave an offering that was personally meaningful to the person whose grave you are visiting, such as a favorite book.

You can also visit graves that seem to have been abandoned or do not have visitors. Check with the person running the cemetery if you can leave offerings at these graves. Even if you cannot always do so, tending the graves and clearing them of fallen leaves and other debris is a good way to honor the forgotten dead.

In the late 1800s and early 1900s, it was popular to have picnics in cemeteries to share a meal with the dead. This tradition is banned in many graveyards and cemeteries to protect them against littering. However, you can double-check the rules at the cemetery where your loved one is buried. If it is allowed, you can also consider sharing a small meal near their grave to include their spirit in your meal.

When planning a cemetery or graveyard celebration, check the rules. Some graveyards explicitly prohibit picnicking or eating on the premises, while others limit the types of offerings you can lay on a person's grave. These rules are often meant to protect the graves in the cemetery, so be respectful and tailor your celebration around them.

Perform Bonfire Magic

Samhain is often celebrated with bonfires, making it a good time to practice bonfire magic. This ritual can be performed by independent practitioners and covens and is a perfect addition to any Samhain celebration involving a bonfire.

Once you have a bonfire going, write down a habit you want to free yourself from. Think about your desire to release this habit and imagine yourself adopting healthier habits in the coming New Year.

While doing so, toss the paper with the habit you have written down into the bonfire.

This ritual can also be performed around a fireplace if you cannot host a bonfire outside.

Perform a Ritual to Mark the End of the Harvest

Samhain also marks the end of the harvest season and serves as a welcome to winter, when very little grows. This makes it a key part of the Wheel of the Year, and it is a time to celebrate the abundance the year has given you.

You Will Need:
- An altar decorated with signs of late fall (such as items that symbolize the dead and the spirit world, harvest foods, nuts and berries, dried leaves and acorns, a filled cornucopia, mulled cider/wine/mead, or any other items you find important)
- A loaf of dark bread and apple cider or wine
- The straw you can use to make a straw man or woman

This ritual is ideally performed with family, loved ones, or a coven, though you can modify it for a solo practitioner. You can perform it on a single day or daily for three days, culminating in Samhain.

Instructions:
1. To begin the ritual, prepare a meal for your loved ones. The meal should emphasize the fruit of the recent harvest season, including fruit, vegetables, and wild game meat if possible (and if you consume meat).
2. Decorate the dinner table with candles and a centerpiece that celebrates fall if possible.
3. Before eating, acknowledge the end of the harvest, the coming winter, and the harvest bounty in front of you. Thank the earth for its fruits.
4. Take the cup of cider/wine and guide everyone outside. You can choose any space outside you can all gather in—a vegetable or garden patch would be best, but any area in your front yard will do.
5. Each person involved in the ritual should sprinkle some of the wine/cider on the earth. While doing so, acknowledge the summer that is gone, the winter that is coming, and the end of the harvest.
6. Each person should use straw to make a straw man or woman. Bring it with you as you reenter your home.
7. Place your own straw man/woman at the table with a seat and plate of his/her own. Serve him food first.
8. Break a few crumbs from the dark bread and toss it outside for the birds.

9. Share a meal with your loved ones, keeping the straw man/King of Winter in his place of honor. He should stay there throughout the season. Once the season is over, you should place him in the garden to watch over the new seedlings before burning him in a Beltane ritual.
10. After finishing your meal, put any leftovers in the garden for the animals to eat.
11. Finish the night by celebrating around a bonfire, playing games, or telling scary stories.

This ritual is the perfect time to involve your children in your practice. They can help you gather the fruit and vegetables for the meal, make the King of Winter from straw, and feed the birds and other animals with bread crumbs and leftovers. Explain the importance of the harvest and sharing your bounty with other creatures while you do so, and explain why honoring the King of Winter is as important as celebrating the fall and the harvest season.

Ritual to Honor Lost Loved Ones

You can perform this relatively simple ritual with children, other loved ones, and coven members. It is a good option for practitioners performing a ritual for the first time and those who want something that children can be involved in from start to finish.

For this ritual, you should set up your Samhain altar with the help of your children. If they are too young to use candles safely, you can add LED candles and tea lights instead.

Ask your children—and other friends, family, and coven members—if there are people they would like to include on the altar. This can include pets and other animals they may have had a bond with. You should also add some photos and mementos of loved ones who have gone before you.

You Will Need:

- An empty plate (to pass around)
- Food to use as an offering (something plain, like bread, so that children are not tempted to eat it during the ritual instead)

- A cup with a drink in it that everyone can share (this can be milk, cider, or any other drink that both adults and children can have. If you are not comfortable sharing a cup, you can also use individual cups or glasses)

Start the ritual by casting a circle if doing so is a part of your normal practice.

Instructions:
1. Ask everyone to gather around the altar and take a few moments to think about the family members and loved ones each of you has lost. For children too young to know a deceased loved one, ask them to think about living the family members and others who are important to them. Reassure them that thinking about a lost pet is okay, too.
2. Start the ritual by acknowledging the importance of Samhain and your celebration of the people you have lost. Vocally acknowledge each person you will honor, starting with those who have recently died. You do not need to recite entire genealogies, but you should acknowledge those most important to you. If you want, you can add information about who each person/pet was. Others can join in with their acknowledgments.
3. Once you have all acknowledged people you have lost, pass the plate around with the food offerings on it. Each person should take a little.
4. Once each member has an offering, you should approach the altar one at a time, working your way from the oldest to the youngest. Leave your offering on the altar in a dedicated bowl/plate.
5. Ask everyone to pray to the gods or deities they follow or your ancestors, acknowledging their importance and asking them to share in the offerings. For smaller children, this can be as simple as just saying "Thank you"—you can say this on behalf of the littlest ones if need be.
6. Pass the cup around—or ask everyone to get their cups. Take a sip in honor of your ancestors, acknowledging this fact as you do so. If you are passing around a single cup, invite the person you are passing it to share in the drink.

7. Place the cup on the altar when everyone has had a sip. If you use individual cups, place a single cup on the altar. Join hands, close your eyes, and acknowledge and thank your ancestors. Take a moment to reflect quietly on your loved ones before ending the ritual in your preferred manner—sharing a meal with your loved ones if possible.

Other ways to celebrate Samhain, focusing on the spiritual side of things, include spells, charms, baths, prayers, and blessings. The next two chapters will cover all these topics, ensuring you're ready for everything Samhain brings.

Chapter 9: Spells, Charms, and Baths

Spell preparation.
https://pixabay.com/images/id-5659775/

Samhain is the spiritual gate between the lighter and darker parts of the year. It is also a divider between our past and present. With the veil between the worlds made thinner—and us being able to communicate with the inhabitants of the spiritual world at this time of the year—anything becomes possible. However, to learn from the past and for us to invite our ancestors, deities, and other spiritual allies, we sometimes need a little help from nature's magic. This chapter's spells, charms, and baths are designed to bring forth this magic and enhance your powers. With their help, you will receive messages from the spiritual world and interpret them correctly.

You'll also charge your heart with power and gain the ability to bring love into your life. After all, love is the core of every human relationship. All of us are motivated by love in one way or another. However, all love spells and charms should only be cast between consensual parties. You should never cast any spell on others without them approving it first, and, above all, all spells and charms are meant to be positive activities you can participate in during Samhain. They should never be used as part of dark magic rituals. You can use smudging, incense, or anything else you feel necessary to banish negativity from your space and attract all the positive energy you need for your Samhain celebration. To avoid mixing negative energy into them, even accidentally, make sure you cleanse your space before performing any spells.

Ancestor Inviting Spell

Ancestral spirits can be your greatest source of wisdom.

You will need:

- Several black and white candles
- A container
- A representation of your ancestors on your altar or sacred place
- Your spell

To enact this spell:

- At night, when the moon is high, turn off all your lights and place one candle in the center of your altar, with the others around it.
- Light the main candle while reciting the following spell:

"With this light, I invite you (the name of your ancestors) and ask you to join me to celebrate this magical night.

I welcome my departed loved ones into this home and honor their presence amongst us."

- If you are working in a group, each person involved in the ritual should light one of the remaining candles while sharing something about one of the ancestors you have invited.
- If you are working alone, you can remember each ancestor with a sentence or two, depending on how much time you have.
- When the candles have burned down, thank your ancestors for joining you on this night.

A Simple Samhain Wish Spell

With this straightforward spell, you can make all your wishes come true at Samhain. It is performed during the night and only requires one ingredient.

You will need:

- A glass of juice (preferably organic)

To enact this spell:

1. Pour a glass of organic juice and take it outside. If you cannot leave your home, stand at your window so that you can look at the moon.
2. Set your gaze on the moon and tell her what you wish for. Make sure that you paint as detailed a picture as possible.
3. Raise your glass to the moon and recite the following:

"Goddess of the Moon, look and see

This drink that I offer thee

It is yours for all you do

O benevolent one of bright hue."

4. Pour the juice on the ground and thank the moon for her assistance. Your wish will be granted soon.

A Spell for Releasing the Past

This spell is perfect for releasing all the pent-up emotions you harbor due to past traumatic experiences. With them, you will also banish the harmful energy from your body, liberating your inner power.

You will need:
- A pen
- Paper
- 1 candle or bonfire.

To enact this spell:
1. Make a list of negative emotions you wish to banish from within yourself. They can be related to people, events, or anything else that brings up harmful feelings.
2. Go outside and either light a bonfire or candle. You can also light a candle in your home—just make sure you have the moon in your sights.
3. Look up at the moon and then look down at your paper and read the list aloud.
4. Put your list into the fire to burn it while reciting the following:

"*With this fire, I banish anything harmful.*
Now my mind and spirit will be clean,
And I will renew my strength from within."

Dream Ancestor Connection

This is another simple spell to invite your ancestors to join you in your Samhain celebration—this time in your dreams.

You will need:
- Paper
- A pen
- A representation of your ancestor
- A comfortable bed

To enact this spell:
- Before you go to bed on Samhain, say the name of the ancestor you want to connect with in your dreams.
- Hold their picture or personal item that symbolizes your connection to them while saying the following:

"*My beloved (ancestor's name or relation to you)*
I invite you into my dreams tonight
to ask you for your advice.
I require your strength and wisdom
for only this can provide me guidance."

- Leave a piece of paper and a pen by your bed—in case you wake up during the night and want to write down the message your ancestor sent you.
- Lie down, close your eyes, and wait for your dream—and your ancestor—to come.

A Spell for Abundance

This spell will help you invite luck into your life at Samhain. This luck will accompany you through the rest of the year, filling your life with an abundance of everything you need. You will gain everything you desire, even if it takes time.

You will need:
- A candle
- A pendant
- String

To enact this spell:
- Loop the string around the pendant and secure it by tying it before lighting the candle.
- Hold the pendant above the flame and start moving it back and forth while chanting the following:

"*As this candle flickers, this pendant will pass good energy and fortune to me.*

I will gain wealth, power, knowledge, and influence.
This pendant I will pass into power,
to attract wealth, power, and influence, come to me!"

- Repeat the spell three times, and then tie the string around your neck to keep this new source of energy close to your body.
- Wear the pendant until you feel life is filled with all the abundance you need, occasionally recasting the spell whenever you feel low on luck.

A Spell to Deepen Love Between Two People

While you cannot create love out of anything, you can use this spell to deepen the connection between you and your loved one if the sentiment is already there.

You will need:

- 2 red apples
- 1 pink or red candle
- Pink or red string
- A Pen
- Paper

To enact this spell:

1. Place your candle on your altar or table and light it.
2. Take the pen and paper and write down your name and your loved one's name.
3. Fold the piece of paper into a square, hiding the names.
4. Cut the apples in half, and place one half from each apple in front of you.
5. Put the folded piece of paper between the two apple halves while holding these closely together.
6. Take your string and tie it around both apple halves to keep them firmly embraced.

7. Take your apple outside and bury it in your garden while reciting these words:

"Our love is bound by this spell.

As the passion burns through us

and kindness rushes through us,

Our love is forever bound by this spell."

8. Let your candle burn all the way, and do not forget to say thanks to nature once you start to feel the deepening of your relationship.

A Spell to Sever Ties with Your Past

Sometimes, the only way to re-invite positive energy into your life and magical practice is to completely sever ties with someone or something that hurt you in the past.

You will need:
- A piece of black string
- A small black candle
- A fireproof container
- Tape
- Scissors

To enact this spell:
1. Place your candle in the container and light it.
2. Use the tape to secure one end of the black string at one side of the container's rim and the other end on the other side.
3. Close your eyes and envision this string symbolizing your connection to the person, event, or item harmed in the past.
4. When you feel ready, use your scissors to cut the string right down the middle while imagining that you are also severing all emotional ties with the harmful entity.
5. Now, recite the following:

"*I hereby release this from my heart,*

as it no longer belongs there.

The new connection, I invite in its place.

An emotion that is true and fair."

6. Place the container outside your home or on your windowsill.
7. Allow the candle to burn down and enjoy being free from all the negativity caused by whatever you just severed ties with.

A Protection Charm against Unwanted Spirits

Unfortunately, among those spirits that cross the divide at Samhain, there are also harmful spirits you want to stay far away from. Use this charm to keep unwanted spirits away from you and your loved ones.

You will need:

- Rosemary
- 1 clove of garlic
- Salt
- A black stone
- A red cloth
- Black cord
- A picture of the fifth pentacle of the moon

To enact this spell:

- Mix the rosemary with salt, and imbue the mixture with your intention.
- Pour the mixture upon the red cloth you have placed on your altar or sacred place beforehand.
- Add the garlic clove to the mixture and take the black stone into your hands. Envision its protective energy traveling toward you and uniting with your intention of keeping unwanted spirits at bay.
- As soon as you feel this energy encompassing your body, lower the stone onto the herbs.
- Take the representation of the fifth pentacle of the moon and fold it in half by holding it away from your body. This will send the negativity away from you.
- Place the folded picture on the herbs and stone.
- Join the four corners of the cloth at the center and secure them with the black cord. Make sure you tie a triple knot for added security but leave enough cord—you'll need it to

hang up the charm.

- Step outside with the charm in your hand and prepare to place it on your front door by taking a deep breath and envisioning the desired outcome.
- At this point, you should sense a barrier that will allow you to keep unwanted spirits away from your home but that enables you to grant those who wish to invite permission. When you do, repeat the following spell:

"On Samhain night, as all spirits roam,
I cast this spell with herb and stone,
While spirits will wander from their eternal home,
from their spectral haunt, I shall seal my home.
And by hanging this charm,
I'll receive no harm."

- Hang your newly empowered charm on your door and let it do its job. It will protect you on the night of Samhain and keep away any lingering malicious spirits that may have stayed in this world after the veil has been restored.
- You may dispose of the charm anytime you feel that you do not need any additional protection.

Samhain Cleansing Bath Spell

Take this bath on the night of Samhain to banish negative energy from your life and manifest your wishes through your inner power.

You will need:

- Black, white, blue, and purple candles (to represent death, life, the god, and goddess)
- Epsom salt and sea salt
- Food coloring (of your choice)
- Essential oils with refreshing scents (such as eucalyptus and citronella)
- Incense (of your choice)
- Moisturizing oil

- Black, white, blue, and purple crystals

To enact this spell:
- Fill your tub with water and add the oils, the food coloring, and the salts.
- Stir the water clockwise to ensure all the ingredients bend together.
- Light the candles and put them at the four corners of your bathtub. While doing this, say the following:

"With this bath, I cleanse my body, soul, and mind,
I am leaving everything that hinders me behind."

- Now place your crystal around the candles and light your incense.
- Enter the bath and let it relax you. Then affirm your intention by inviting the god and the goddess of the moon to help you cleanse yourself.
- Call upon the four elements of nature to lend their power to you. Then remember your living loved ones through the white candle and the dead ones through the black one.
- Close your eyes and envision negative energy leaving your body, mind, and soul. See it enter the water and evaporate from your life through its steam.
- Lie still until you feel cleansed from negativity, and then wash your body.
- When finished, rinse yourself while stating:

"I am now clean of any negativity or harmful spells cast upon me."

- Get out of the bath, dry yourself with a towel, and moisten your body with oil.

Samhain Beauty Spell

Baths are not the only tools for cleansing your body and soul from negative energy. This simple Samhain spell will help you find the beauty from within, filling your life with positivity and encouraging you to chase dreams.

You will need:

- A mirror
- Moonlight
- A picture of whatever physical characteristic you want to enhance
- A pink candle
- Incense (of your choice)

To enact this spell:

- On the night of Samhain, when the moon is high, take a mirror and walk outside. If you cannot go out, you can open a window to see the moon reflected in the mirror.
- Place the picture on the mirror while saying:

"Sacred moon of Samhain, let the wind carry your light,

let your glow surround my body, and let your shine guide my eyes."

- Repeat this three times and concentrate on the body part you want to change. Then say:

"Sacred moon of Samhain, shape and mold my body,

as a rose is granted a blossoming beauty, let me thrive in your light,

the light that brings me the power of beauty and grants it three times three."

- Repeat this three times as well, and light the pink candle or incense when you have finished.

Chapter 10: Samhain Prayers and Blessings

Apart from rituals and spells connected to the season, your practice can also benefit from uplifting prayers, particularly when celebrating the pagan sabbat of Samhain. This chapter includes various types of prayers and blessings for this holiday. Some are designed to honor your ancestors and the Celtic deities, while others are more about celebrating life around the traditional harvest season. You can also use them during meditation or whenever you need to draw strength during your days at this time of the year. You will also receive a few practical tips for personalizing your prayers and blessings according to your spiritual beliefs. This will help you find a way to take advantage of this holiday, whether your journey takes you toward Druidry, Wicca, or any other form of paganism.

A Prayer for Bountiful Harvest

Whether you wish for plenty of healthy crops in your garden or enjoy a productive harvest in any other area of your life, reciting this prayer at Samhain will help you achieve it. It honors the dying earth that gave its life during harvest to nourish everyone in need. While it will lay dormant in the winter, the prayer will remind you that nature will continue its cycle in the spring.

To ensure nature brings you a plentiful harvest again at every Samhain, say the following prayer:

"The corn has been gathered,
the grain is being prepared, and
the healing herbs are now drying.
Our grapes have been pressed,
our potatoes unearthed, and
our beans are already canned.
After this harvest season,
may our food be ready for winter.
May our souls be ready to give and receive
So, we can eat and live gratefully
for whatever we may have in the following months."

Pagan Ancestor Prayer for Samhain

As you know, during Samhain, the veil between our world and the world of spirits is thinner than ever, which is the best time to communicate with your ancestors. This prayer will help you honor your bloodline so that they can aid you on your life's journey in the coming year. With this prayer, you can express gratitude for the wisdom of those who lived before you—as they made you who you are.

Try to relax your mind as you would do during meditation or yoga, and repeat the following:

"At the night of Samhain, when the divide between the world is thinnest
I call out to those who lived and experienced before me.
Tonight, I honor my ancestors, calling to anyone who carried my blood.
I welcome my ancestors to join me at Samhain
and watch over me tonight and always,
protecting me from bad spirits and guiding me through life.
Tonight, I thank you for the blood that runs in my veins,
for it carries your spirit, which fills my heart,

and tonight, I thank you and will always remember you..."

At this point, you may want to mention the name of a few of your ancestors. Then continue:

"*So, with the gift of remembrance*
My dead will never be forgotten,
as they live within me,
and within those yet to come."

Wiccan Samhain Blessing

The following blessing is widely popular among Wiccans who wish to be protected from ancestral spirits and, at the same time, express their gratitude while being blessed.

Repeat the following blessing to protect yourself and your loved ones at Samhain:

"*On Samhain's Eve,*
May our ancestors protect you,
from darkness and malicious spirits among us,
Before the new year begins,
While the old one is saying goodbye,
We honor our dead and old.
To express our gratitude for the bountiful harvest,
we offer it to our ancestors so that they can watch over us,
They'll keep us away from harm,
As we enter the new cycle of life."

Ancient Celtic Samhain Blessing

This is another traditional Samhain blessing that is a homage to the ancestors—only this one originates from the ancient Celtic pagan era. During this period, people expressed their respect for the end of nature's life cycle, which symbolizes letting go of the past and focusing on the future.

Recite the following blessing to honor your Celtic ancestors:

"*The veil grows thin at this time, and the dead come closer to us,*
We honor them, and we remember those whose footsteps we

tread.
>   As life around us retreats into the bulbs and the roots,
>   where it waits for the time to pass to bring the flowers and fruits.
>   As leaves fall and cover the ground,
>   Mother Nature awaits in stillness profound.
>   As time stands still for all creatures,
>   We prepare many feasts.
>   We seek the wisdom of those gone by,
>   And ask for help with how to deal with the past.
>   May we face our shadows and accept our faults,
>   and may we look now to the future to seek new goals."

Wiccan Food Blessing

This traditional blessing is used to bless the food. For pagans, it doubles as an expression of gratitude for the great harvest and whatever gifts this season may bring.

Here is how to bless your meals when celebrating Samhain:

> "*May we be blessed with a fruitful harvest,*
> *As the earth quickly turns into darkness,*
> *Blessed be the meal we prepare for family and friends,*
> *For all the abundance of fruits, roots, and bread,*
> *Blessed be nature, who nurtures us with care,*
> *We give our thanks to Samhain and all the crops we gathered.*
> *We wish everyone a blessed Samhain!"*

Samhain Prayers for Druids

The following prayers are often recited by Druids, who have a unique way of honoring Samhain and the wonderful benefits this sabbat provides for pagan practices.

Typically, Druids open all Samhain celebrations with the following prayer:

> "*O great spirits, of the land which upholds us,*
> *the sky that embraces us, and the sea that grounds us.*

*As we stay in the center as living fire,
let our work be done as we wish to do it."*

Grounding for Inspiration

Druids place much emphasis on grounding themselves when seeking inspiration. This prayer will help you with that. Envision your past as a maze of underground roots, representing the foundation of your being. Feel how the roots are grounding you—and how they are always there for you, nourishing you throughout your life's journey.

Light a fire, and when you are ready, you can call upon inspiration from your roots with the following Druidic prayer:

"*Our poets, our ancient wordsmiths,
Collect the ancient staves of Knowledge,
And let the eloquence light the fire in our minds."*

You may offer tree branches, fruit, dry crops, or anything else you may want to use to the fire while reciting this prayer.

Honoring the Tuatha

As the most influential Celtic spirits, the Tuatha will always be there to help pagans out, which is why Druids often turned to them for guidance. Honoring them with blessings and prayers at Samhain will ensure they hear your call. This can be done either over a fire, water, or a sacred tree.

To do it over the fire, recite the following while anointing your flames with oil or butter:

"*O sacred fire of Samhain that transforms me,
let its flame warm my spirit and enlighten my life.
Relight the sacred flames that burn within me,
bring the Tuatha to me."*

If you want to do it over water, you will need to say the following while dropping a coin into a sacred well:

"*O sacred waters that flow beneath the earth,
help me understand the fluid depths within myself.
To uncover the sacred well that flows within me,*

bring the Tuatha to me."

Doing it over a sacred tree will require you to take a branch of the tree and recite the following over it:

"O sacred tree that stands between the realms of land, sky, and sea,

let me feel the power of your depths,

Let me be empowered by your strength.

Revive the sacred tree that thrives within me; bring the Tuatha to me."

Calling on Brigid

Brigid is the pagan goddess who can open many gates and accompany you on your journey, aiding you whenever you need it. You may call upon her at Samhain with this praise:

"O Brigid, sacred goddess of the gates of wisdom,

may I walk on your path as I explore mine."

Repeat this several times while tending to a fire or gazing into a well. As the goddess of domesticity, these are the places where you can easily connect with Brigid. You may also make her an offering to make the prayer even more effective.

Inviting Other Beings

Apart from Brigid, Druids may call other beings living in the spiritual world to their side at Samhain. Badb, Anand, Macha, Airmed, Miach, and Lugh are just some of the ancient Celtic pagan ancestors that can come to someone's aid. Druids can also invite their immediate blood ancestors if they need more of their teachings.

If you decide to go down the latter path, you may do so with the following Druid prayer:

"I call out to my closest ancestors

Those whose blood I carry.

I call out to the ancestors we all learned from.

I call out to the ancestors who rest in this land.

I call out to the ancestors of my blood, heart, and bone and offer you welcome.

I call you as my kin, meet me at the boundary of the worlds, and accept my offering!"

Make an offering to the ancestors. Then continue with the following:

"I call out to the spirits of all the worlds.

I call out to my allies from the sacred land of spirits.

I call out to the spirits of my land and home,

of the mighty sea and vast sky, and offer you welcome.

I call you as my kin, meet me at the boundary of the worlds, and accept my offering!"

After the ritual, make an offering to the spirits, too.

Prayer of Sacrifice

At Samhain, a prayer of sacrifice will also bring you closer to the spirits living in the otherworld. You should include an intention that expresses your willingness to share hospitality to form an alliance with these spirits.

For example, your prayer can read something like this:

"I invite you to the sacred place I have established for us.

I have brought the worlds together and have summoned your spirits,

As well as the spirits of my ancestors and their gods.

Please come to a place you won't find anywhere else, at any time.

Join now the gathering of gods, the dead, and of sidhe.

I offer you this gift so that I might receive your guidance, should you wish to grant it.

Let my voice arise from this sacred fire,

let my voice carry on into the depths I aspire,

may the spirits accept my offerings,

Their ways are the only ones I keep.

Accept my Sacrifice!"

At this point, you show the ancestors the sacred place you have set up for them and the offerings you've made. You ask them to sit with you at this place so that you can entertain them throughout the night by telling stories and singing folk songs. Before parting from the spirits, recite the farewell poem, or speak to them about the quiet joys of kinship.

Divination Prayer

This prayer should be recited for divination, typically combined with other tools you would use for foretelling.

For example, Druids often cast ogham for divination by saying:

"*The few of us fill a future as fated foreseen,*

as we ignore the fights of our foes' fury.

May we foretell the fool's failure, warn of fame,

and predict who may be granted flawless flourish for playing a fair game."

In the end, you should speak an interpretation of what you have seen when casting the ogham.

Closing Prayer

Just as Druids use an opening prayer to commence their rituals, they would also conclude their affairs with a meaningful closing prayer. After making new contacts with the Celtic deities and finding new ways to honor ancestral spirits or make good on your old connections, you should recite the following:

"*Wave your hand over the flame.*

Let the fire be but flame.

Wave your hand over the water.

Let the well be but water.

Wave your hand over the tree.

Let all be as it was before; let the ways be closed!"

Personalizing Samhain Blessings and Prayers

Samhain is a time for remembrance, honoring the dead, and letting go of past grievances. All these activities require a deep connection with your spiritual self—something each of us has unique ways of achieving. For this reason, while the prayers and blessings in this chapter could be a great stepping stone for your journey as they are, it is always a good idea to add your individual touch to them. Remember, pagan practices are about what feels right to you. Samhain is also the time of the year when many empowering spells are cast and divinations made. This is another powerful reason to personalize the prayers and blessings you recite during this sabbat.

One way to personalize Samhain prayers is by inviting your loved ones to participate in them. Even if they are not pagan practitioners, being invited to a Samhain-themed supper can get them in the mood for saying a prayer or blessing. This is particularly true if you display a picture or mementos of the dearly departed you were all fond of.

Lighting candles is another way to make a Samhain blessing your own. Candle flame can be the perfect alternative to the traditional Samhain bonfires if you cannot attend one. Light candles in the color of Samhain—black, white, blue, and purple—or whatever color you prefer before reciting your blessing. This will get you in the mood for making a spiritual connection. You can also use crystals in the same colors to further enhance the effect.

You may also pour a small amount of beer, wine, or any special drink you have on hand for Samhain into a glass or goblet. Offering this to the dead upon your altar or table when saying a prayer or blessing is another spin on the traditional Pagan custom.

If you live in a larger community, you can share your way of celebrating Samhain with others. Pagan prayers are typically accompanied by offerings, oaths, healing, divination, or other rites of magic. Thus, what better way to empower these than sharing the flame that connects you to the spirit of Samhain? Larger pagan communities often light a central fire—and the individual members take coal from it to relight their hearth after extinguishing it during this sabbat. If you are a solitary practitioner, you can always envision a perpetual flame and focus on this when relighting your fire and saying a blessing or prayer.

Giving to the less fortunate has always been part of the ancient Samhain tradition. It does not matter how much you have to offer. Whether you celebrate with a large community or not, you can always find someone whom you can share food and other small offerings. If you have the means, you can also help someone with greater needs than yourself. Even if you do not have the means, treating an elderly neighbor to a meal will lift their spirits and yours, too. The possibilities for giving and helping people on Samhain are endless—and doing this at Samhain while reciting a traditional blessing will return to you with unmatched benefits.

Conclusion

As one of the most well-known pagan sabbats, Samhain has always been celebrated with great spiritual conventions and lavish festivities. Its historical connections to the ancient Celtic pagan culture are undeniable, but so are its ties to the modern traditions of Halloween. Throughout the many years it has been celebrated, Samhain has evolved to fit the needs of those who follow the ancient customs and modern Wiccans or Druids alike. With so many symbols, herbs, candles, stones, and other tools available for you to honor Samhain, you can celebrate this magical time of the year in a manner that seems right to you.

You have learned about the deities and spirits associated with this holiday. You have also discovered what this time of the year ultimately represents: The gateway between life and death. At Samhain, the veil between our world and the spiritual world is at its thinnest. You can invite any helpful soul through it to your side—from the crones and goddesses living in the spiritual world and helping those who cross find peace with your long-lost ancestors to malicious spirits; the remnants of those who could not find peace may also cross the divide. Thus, you must be careful with your spiritual practices at this time of the year. Fortunately, with proper preparation, you can gain power and wisdom from the spirits with a positive influence and protect yourself and your loved ones from harm.

While setting up an altar is not required for practicing magic at Samhain, creating this sacred place can help you focus your mind on your intention and the tools you use for each spell or ritual. Whether you are familiar with spiritual practices or are just delving into them, there are plenty of Samhain-themed crafts and decorations to make to get into the spirit of the sabbat. Creating them may also relax you, serving as mental preparation for cleansing yourself and your space so only positive energy can remain.

Make sure you prepare lots of herbs and plants with healing and cleansing properties as you will need them during your Samhain activities. You may also find it helpful to have crystals at hand. You can draw energy from crystals if you need added support when casting a protection spell or performing a divination ritual. Choose stones in the same colors as the candles you'll be using—the traditional colors of Samhain. Do not forget to gather some essential oils for your cleansing bath, which you'll take on the full moon of Samhain.

The spells, rituals, blessings, and prayers you have found in this book can be incorporated into your Samhain activities, regardless of your pagan practices. You can even personalize them further to ensure they bring you the most benefits. Some you might take on your pagan journey even after this sabbat has passed. You can also introduce them to your family, encouraging them to participate in the preparations and the festivities. Whether they belong to the pagan community or have a different spiritual background, they will be happy to recite prayers or blessings with you—especially those created to honor your common ancestors or bring love and abundance to all. And, if nothing else, your friends and family are sure to enjoy preparing some delicious traditional Samhain meals and implementing them into their customs.

Here's another book by Mari Silva that you might like

Your Free Gift (only available for a limited time)

Thanks for getting this book! If you want to learn more about various spirituality topics, then join Mari Silva's community and get a free guided meditation MP3 for awakening your third eye. This guided meditation mp3 is designed to open and strengthen ones third eye so you can experience a higher state of consciousness. Simply visit the link below the image to get started.

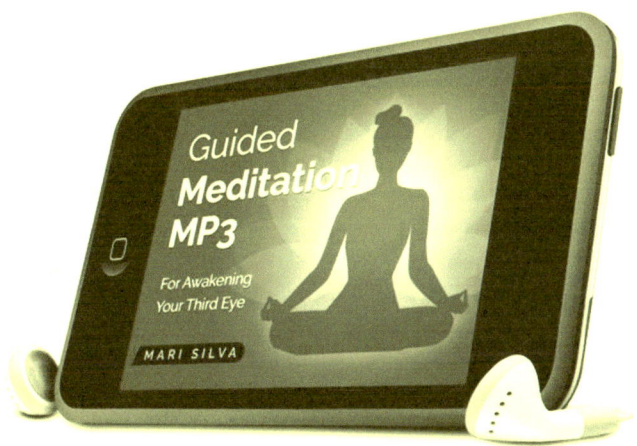

https://spiritualityspot.com/meditation

Bibliography

Altar and Oddity. (2020, December 21). *Sacred spaces: How to make an altar in your home.* https://altarandoddity.com/blogs/news/sacred-spaces-how-to-make-an-altar

Apel, T. (2022, April 28). *Pluto.* Mythopedia. https://mythopedia.com/topics/pluto

Barry, B. (2019, October 31). *Samhain and the thin veil.* Donegal Square. https://donegalsquare.com/samhain-and-the-thin-veil/

Browne, N. (2021, December 22). *Arawn: The Celtic god of death and the underworld, explained.* Ireland Before You Die. https://www.irelandbeforeyoudie.com/arawn-the-celtic-god-of-death-and-the-underworld-explained/

Cartwright, M. (2013, September 22). *Mictlantecuhtli.* World History Encyclopedia. https://www.worldhistory.org/Mictlantecuhtli/

Clever Prototypes, L. L. C. (n.d.). *Rhea: Greek mythology.* Accessed July 1, 2022. https://www.storyboardthat.com/mythology/rhea

Cline, A. (2019, February 17). *Mictlantecuhtli: God of death in Aztec religion.* Learn Religions https://www.learnreligions.com/mictlantecuhtli-god-aztec-of-death-248588

Daimler, M. (2016, October 18). *Irish-American witchcraft: The Morrigan and Samhain.* Patheos. https://www.patheos.com/blogs/agora/2016/10/irish-american-witchcraft-the-morrigan-and-samhain/

The Editors of Encyclopedia Britannica. (2022, March 28). *Zeus.* Encyclopedia Britannica. https://www.britannica.com/topic/Zeus

The Editors of GreekMythology.com. (2018, March 13). *Dionysus*. Greekmythology.com. https://www.greekmythology.com/Other_Gods/Dionysus/dionysus.html

The Editors of GreekMythology.com. (2021, April 9). *Hecate*. GreekMythology.com https://www.greekmythology.com/Other_Gods/Hecate/hecate.html#:~:text=Hecate%20was%20a%20goddess%20in,protective%20goddess%20who%20brought%20prosperity.

The Editors of GreekMythology.com. (2021, October 6). *Hermes*. Greekmythology.com. GreekMythology.com. https://www.greekmythology.com/Olympians/Hermes/hermes.html

Enodian, R. (2018, October 22). *Celebrating Hermes, messenger god & guide of souls, on Samhain*. Patheos. https://www.patheos.com/blogs/teaaddictedwitch/2018/10/celebrating-hermes-samhain/

Enodian, R. (2018, October 13). *Descent and ascent: Persephone claiming her throne at Samhain*. Patheos. https://www.patheos.com/blogs/teaaddictedwitch/2018/10/ascent-descent-persephone-samhain/

Ethical Gains. (2020, October 20). *What is Samhain? The history of the pagan celebration*. Sea Witch Botanicals. https://seawitchbotanicals.com/blogs/swb/what-is-samhain-the-history-of-the-pagan-celebration

Fox, C. (2018). *Hades*. Bantam.

Frasca, C. (2021, October 7). *Cerridwen's cauldron and the origins of Samhain by Caireann Frasca*. Motherhouse of the Goddess. http://themotherhouseofthegoddess.com/2021/10/07/cerridwens-cauldron-and-the-origins-of-samhain-by-caireann-frasca/

Gaia Staff. (2021, October 29). *Samhain rituals – How to celebrate Samhain*. Gaia. https://www.gaia.com/article/modern-paganism-13-rituals-celebrate-samhain

The Goddess and the Greenman. (2021, October 4). *Samhain/Halloween October 31st*. https://www.goddessandgreenman.co.uk/samhainhalloween/

Goddess Garden. (2018, December 17). *The Celtic goddess Cerridwen*. The Goddess Garden. https://thegoddessgarden.com/the-celtic-goddess-cerridwen/

Greek Gods and Goddesses. (2014, September 19). *Hades (Haides)*. https://greekgodsandgoddesses.net/gods/hades/

Greeley, S. (2021, October 6). *From Samhain to Halloween: The history of Halloween traditions*. Little Rae's Bakery. https://littleraesbakery.com/2021/10/06/from-samhain-to-halloween-the-history-of-halloween-traditions/

Helena. (2021, January 24). *How to build an altar at home for spiritual self-care*. Disorient. https://disorient.co/build-an-altar/

History.com Editors. (2009, November 18). *Halloween 2021*. HISTORY. https://www.history.com/topics/halloween/history-of-halloween

History.com Editors. (2018, April 6). *Samhain*. HISTORY. https://www.history.com/topics/holidays/samhain

Hurstwic, LLC. (n.d.). *The death of Baldr*. Accessed July 1, 2022. http://www.hurstwic.org/history/articles/mythology/myths/text/baldr.htm

Johannesen, H. (2013, September 21). *Hekate: Goddess of Samhain*. Eternal Haunted Summer. https://eternalhauntedsummer.com/issues/autumn-equinox-2013/hekate-goddess-of-samhain/

Johnson, E. (2018, July 24). *A salute to the seasons: Creating seasonal altars*. WomanShopsWorld. https://shopwomanshopsworld.com/blogs/womanshopsworld-blog/a-salute-to-the-seasons-creating-seasonal-altars

Julian, J. A. (2014, September 30). *Samhain symbols – Animals*. The Pagan Circle. https://thepagancircle.wordpress.com/2014/09/30/samhain-symbols-animals/

Keith, J. (2019, October 13). *Halloween plant lore*. Fafard. https://fafard.com/halloween-plant-lore/

ladyoftheabyss. (2018, October 27). *Samhain goddesses – Hel – Norse*. Witches Of The Craft®. https://witchesofthecraft.com/2018/10/27/samhain-goddesses-hel-norse/

Lang, C. (2018, October 30). *What is Samhain? What to know about the ancient pagan festival that came before Halloween*. Time USA, LLC. https://time.com/5434659/halloween-pagan-origins-in-samhain/

Larson, C. (2019, October 13). *Of light & shadow: Connecting with Anubis at Samhain*. Patheos. https://www.patheos.com/blogs/agora/2019/10/of-light-shadow-connecting-with-anubis-at-samhain/

Larson, C. (2018, October 23). *'Samhain' in ancient Egypt?* Of Light & Shadow. https://anubislightandshadow.wordpress.com/2018/10/23/samhain-in-ancient-egypt/

Locatelli-Kournwsky, L. (2018). *Persephone*. Archaia Studios Press.

Mackay, D. (2021, June 27). *Everything you need to know about Hecate (maiden, mother, crone)*. TheCollector. https://www.thecollector.com/hecate-goddess-magic-witchcraft/

Mankey, J. (2018, October 18). *Samhain deities*. Patheos. https://www.patheos.com/blogs/panmankey/2018/10/samhain-deities/

Marie, M. (2020, October 13). *What is the story of the ancient Pharaonic deity Anubis?* Egypttoday. https://www.egypttoday.com/Article/4/93038/What-is-the-story-of-the-ancient-Pharaonic-deity-Anubis

Mark, J. J. (2021, September 6). *Hel*. World History Encyclopedia. https://www.worldhistory.org/Hel/

McGinley, K. (2019, September 16). *Sacred space: How to make an altar in your home*. Chopra. https://chopra.com/articles/sacred-space-how-to-make-an-altar-in-your-home

McLeod, H. (2021, October 27). *Samhain and the history of Halloween*. The Smoky Mountain News. https://smokymountainnews.com/lifestyle/rumble/item/32445-samhain-and-the-history-of-halloween

Meehan, E. (2021, November 20). *Huitzilopochtli*. Mythopedia. https://mythopedia.com/topics/huitzilopochtli

Meehan, E. (2021, November 20). *Mictlantecuhtli*. Mythopedia. https://mythopedia.com/topics/mictlantecuhtli

Meehan, E. (2021, November 20). *Quetzalcoatl*. Mythopedia. https://mythopedia.com/topics/quetzalcoatl

Meehan, E. (2021, November 20). *Tezcatlipoca*. Mythopedia. https://mythopedia.com/topics/tezcatlipoca

Meehan, E. (2021, November 20). *Xipe Totec*. Mythopedia. https://mythopedia.com/topics/xipe-totec

Mojsov, B. (Ed.). (2005). *Osiris*. Blackwell Publishing Ltd.

Moonshadow. (2021, October 29). *Hecate and Samhain*. Spells8 Forum. https://forum.spells8.com/t/hecate-and-samhain/15764

Myth Nerd. (2021, March 20). *Anubis and Osiris: What is the difference?* https://mythnerd.com/anubis-and-osiris-what-is-the-difference/

Neshevich, V. (2020, October 28). *Five important crystals for Samhain*. Green Moon Apothecary Ltd. https://greenmoon.ca/blogs/blog/five-important-crystals-for-samhain

Newgrange.com. (n.d.). *Samhain (Samain) - The Celtic roots of Halloween.* Accessed July 1, 2022. https://www.newgrange.com/samhain.htm

O'Connor, D. (2022, June 27). *An Cailleach - The Irish goddess of the winter and following her trail in Ireland.* IrishCentral. https://www.irishcentral.com/travel/best-of-ireland/cailleach-irish-goddess-winter-trail-ireland

The Order of Bards, Ovates & Druids. (n.d.). *Samhain festival.* Accessed July 1, 2022. https://druidry.org/druid-way/teaching-and-practice/druid-festivals/samhain-festival

O'Hara, K. (2022, May 26). *The Morrigan goddess: The phantom queen and Celtic goddess (An easy-to-follow tale).* The Irish Road Trip. https://www.theirishroadtrip.com/the-morrigan/

Pon, D. (n.d.). *The origins of Halloween.* Albany.edu. Accessed July 1, 2022. https://www.albany.edu/~dp1252/isp523/halloween.html

Ravenwood, C. (2021). *Celebrating Samhain: A coloring and activity book.* Independently Published.

RaynaNoire.com. (2019, October 29). *Goddesses of Samhain.* http://raynanoire.weebly.com/blog/goddesses-of-samhain

Rhys, D. (n.d.). *Arawn - The Welsh god of the afterlife.* Symbol Sage. Accessed July 1, 2022. https://symbolsage.com/arawn-the-welsh-god/

Rogador, C. (2021, January 29). *Samhain symbol - history and meaning.* Symbols Archive. https://symbolsarchive.com/samhain-symbol-history-meaning/

Russell, T. (2019, January 25). *Why you need a sacred space in your home (& how to create one).* Davy & Tracy Russell. https://davyandtracy.com/spirituality/why-you-need-a-sacred-space-in-your-home/

Sherman, E. (2020, October 23). *How to celebrate pagan Samhain instead of Halloween this year.* Matador Network. https://matadornetwork.com/read/celebrate-wiccan-samhain-instead-halloween-year/

Spookyscotland.net. (2019, October 30). *Halloween origins: Samhain and the Cailleach.* https://spookyscotland.net/the-cailleach/

Stumpp, B. V. (2013, January 15). *The importance of home altars.* Britta's Dance. https://brittasdance.wordpress.com/2013/01/15/the-importance-of-home-altars/

Theoi Project. (n.d.). *Persephone*. Accessed July 1, 2022. https://www.theoi.com/Khthonios/Persephone.html#:~:text=PERSEPHONE%20was%20the%20goddess%20queen,passage%20to%20a%20blessed%20afterlife.

The Thirsty Soul. (2018, October 18). *Samhain: An Cailleach, our ancestors & Celtic New Year*. https://thethirstysoul.com/samhain-an-cailleach-our-ancestors-celtic-new-year/

Ward, K. (2021, August 23). *How to celebrate Samhain, aka the witches' New Year*. Cosmopolitan. https://www.cosmopolitan.com/lifestyle/a34360772/samhain-traditions/

Wigington, P. (2019, January 12). *Cerridwen: Keeper of the cauldron*. Learn Religions. https://www.learnreligions.com/cerridwen-keeper-of-the-cauldron-2561960

Wigington, P. (2019, January 6). *Consecrate your magical tools*. Learn Religions. https://www.learnreligions.com/consecrate-your-magical-tools-2562860

Wigington, P. (2019, August 14). *Sacred plants of the Samhain sabbat*. Learn Religions. https://www.learnreligions.com/sacred-plants-of-the-samhain-sabbat-3879864

Wigington, P. (2019, March 11). *Samhain spirit incense*. Learn Religions. https://www.learnreligions.com/samhain-spirit-incense-4588980

Wigington, P. (2020, April 29). *Setting up your Samhain altar*. Learn Religions. https://www.learnreligions.com/setting-up-a-samhain-altar-2562711

Wigington, P. (2019, June 25). *Set up an ancestor shrine – Ancestor altar*. Learn Religions. https://www.learnreligions.com/ancestor-shrine-ancestor-altar-2562668

Wright, G. (2021, August 27). *Arawn*. Mythopedia. https://mythopedia.com/topics/arawn

Printed by Libri Plureos GmbH in Hamburg, Germany